Life
After Levels

SAGE was founded in 1965 by Sara Miller McCune to support the dissemination of usable knowledge by publishing innovative and high-quality research and teaching content. Today, we publish over 900 journals, including those of more than 400 learned societies, more than 800 new books per year, and a growing range of library products including archives, data, case studies, reports, and video. SAGE remains majority-owned by our founder, and after Sara's lifetime will become owned by a charitable trust that secures our continued independence.

Los Angeles | London | New Delhi | Singapore | Washington DC | Melbourne

Life After Levels

ONE SCHOOL'S STORY OF TRANSFORMING PRIMARY ASSESSMENT

Sam Hunter

Learning Matters
An imprint of SAGE Publications Ltd
1 Oliver's Yard
55 City Road
London EC1Y 1SP

SAGE Publications Inc.
2455 Teller Road
Thousand Oaks, California 91320

SAGE Publications India Pvt Ltd
B 1/I 1 Mohan Cooperative Industrial Area
Mathura Road
New Delhi 110 044

SAGE Publications Asia-Pacific Pte Ltd
3 Church Street
#10-04 Samsung Hub
Singapore 049483

Editor: Amy Thornton
Development Editor: Jennifer Clark
Production Controller: Chris Marke
Project Management: Deer Park Productions
Marketing Manager: Lorna Patkai
Cover design: Wendy Scott
Typeset by: C&M Digitals (P) Ltd, Chennai, India
Printed and bound by CPI Group (UK) Ltd,
Croydon, CR0 4YY

Library of Congress Control Number: 2016940061

British Library Cataloguing in Publication Data

A catalogue record for this book is available from the
British Library

ISBN 978-1-4739-6426-6 paperback
ISBN 978-1-4739-6425-9 hardback

At SAGE we take sustainability seriously. Most of our products are printed in the UK using FSC papers and boards.
When we print overseas we ensure sustainable papers are used as measured by the PREPS grading system.
We undertake an annual audit to monitor our sustainability.

Dedication:

For Simon – I couldn't do this crazy job without you.

C**O**NTENTS

CONTENTS

ABOUT THE AUTHOR

As a headteacher **Sam Hunter** is committed to providing the best possible education to the children in her care. After nearly 20 years working in education, she is currently the head at Hiltingbury Junior School, a thriving learning community in Hampshire, which fosters forward-thinking and outward-looking practice.

In 2014 the school was recognised by the Department for Education through the assessment innovation fund. Since then Sam has been sharing her approach to assessment, while regularly speaking at national conferences and hosting visits to her school. This allows colleagues from across the UK and abroad to experience how *Learning Ladders* works in the classroom.

Sam believes in the power that quality assessment creates for transforming teaching and learning. *Life After Levels* is her first book and her aim is to ensure that schools feel confident in creating their own ethos of assessment, which has pupils' learning at its centre rather than a fear of accountability. She believes that pupils' understanding of their role in learning underpins successful assessment.

Sam is passionate about school-to-school support and is also a guest contributor to *TES*.

ACKNOWLEDGEMENTS

A massive thank you to the amazing learning community of Hiltingbury Junior School. You are inspiring and I can't believe how much we continue to achieve.

Thank you to Matt and the team at School Explained who saw the true vision of Learning Ladders and invested time, passion and understanding into it.

Thank you to my colleagues at Winchester University who thrashed out initial ideas with me and gave me practical advice on publishing a book.

INTRODUCTION

In the autumn of 2013, I became aware of an opportunity for schools to apply for a government grant to invest in developing new assessment ideas for *Life After Levels*. The aim was to provide an opportunity for good practice to be shared as schools stepped into a brave new world of assessment innovation. I was not long into my first headship but I thought I would give it a go. I sat down with a glass of wine one evening and sent in an application. When told we had made it through to short listing I had another glass of Merlot and wrote the more detailed application required for the next stage. Looking back to the day that we were told that we had been successful I remember driving home and thinking, 'Oh my goodness, what have we done?' As a school I had well and truly stuck our heads above the parapet!

However, I am so glad that I did. As daunting, frustrating and exhausting as it is to be shaping something to a tight deadline while being very much in the public eye, the last two years have caused me to really focus on what quality assessment is. The removal of Levels has given all professionals involved in education a unique opportunity to rediscover what we value in this key aspect of teaching and learning. I know that since I qualified in 1997, no government has ever handed over such autonomy to schools (academies and free schools aside) and it is an opportunity that we must grab with both hands. Through the development of Learning Ladders I have needed to reflect on how we have been assessing, why that is and who we are making assessments for. It has challenged my thinking and my practice.

Throughout this book I try to avoid getting on my political soapbox (although it does happen once or twice!). Yes, we are in a period of massive change and flux. In the past months that I have been writing this book the goal posts for the end of key stage assessments, particularly in Writing, have shifted so many times that I have lost count. Yes, the freedom we have been given has been accompanied with confusion and the feeling that the Department for Education is only fractionally ahead of us in its thinking. And yes, there is still no change to the incredible sense of accountability that end of key stage tests bring and the unsustainable pressure that comes with this. Instead, I want this book to provide a time for reflection for teachers and school leaders to re-adjust their thinking on assessment and to get excited about it.

The idea for the Learning Ladders originally came from my maths leader, Sharon Pay, who was frustrated with how we were using maths targets with the children. Unless they were based on using and applying or times tables they were unachievable as the maths topics covered changed so rapidly. It seemed a pointless exercise. She came up with the idea of a Ladder booklet that the children would own. Each key skill in maths would have its own Ladder and the new National Curriculum would be broken down into key objectives, represented by the rungs. As the class moved onto a new skill (Ladder) then target setting for that lesson or unit would focus around the key objectives (rungs). The idea worked so well that we did the same for Reading and Writing. Using the National Curriculum and our professional judgement we agreed end-of-year expectations for Years 1 to 7, as well as for P-Levels.

Our assessment system is based in the classroom. It started with the children and grew from there. Children now understand that there are different skills that are required to become a great reader. They understand that you build on previous learning. They can see the links between Ladders and are motivated to achieve. That has to be a great starting point. The Ladders have facilitated conversations around next steps in learning. They support teachers' planning and inform focused assessment, both within the lessons when we sign off rungs 'live' with the children and also using the online version of Learning Ladders that adds a further layer to our assessment system. The Ladders have also worked as a tool for reporting to parents, both with the children's paper booklets and the online version of Ladders at Home.

Yet in this age of ever-increasing accountability, many school leaders remain tightly focused on tracking. The need for the security of number crunching is so ingrained in what we do that the full scope of what assessment is becomes narrowed down to an obsession with spreadsheets and graphs. The wonderful opportunities that are currently presented to us are in danger of being lost if we simply focus our time and attention on a different system that is still all about the data. The aim of this book is to show life after Levels can also be Life after Tracking.

This book focuses on Key Stage 1 and Key Stage 2 assessment as opposed to Early Years. There simply weren't enough pages to incorporate that too. However, I hope that much of what I talk about will be relevant to colleagues working with Reception classes. Another aspect of assessment that I have not unpicked here is the very specific issue of assessing complex special educational needs, specifically using P-Levels. I believe that the approaches to assessment discussed in these pages are relevant for the vast majority of pupils in mainstream schools and that the principles explored are relevant for all. This book shares the experiences of Hiltingbury Juniors as we have moved away from a Levels system, it presents thinking from past and current educational practitioners and it contains my own thoughts and observations on this topic.

If I were to sum up this book into three words I would choose Opportunity, Re-think and Bravery. There, now you don't have to read it, although I hope you will!

PART ONE
EXPLORING ASSESSMENT

1 ASSESSMENT: WHERE WE ARE NOW (AND HOW WE GOT HERE)

This chapter will:

- consider the current 'situation' of assessment in schools;
- explore recent history of assessment;
- examine where we are now.

INTRODUCTION

Theodore Roosevelt believed that 'the more you know about the past, the better you are prepared for the future'. For this chapter I wish to take the former American president's advice and look at the history of assessment in our schools in this country to help us have a better understanding of where we are with assessment now. When did formal assessment start and in what form? What decisions were made by past politicians and educationalists, and with what motives, that have led us down certain paths over the past centuries? How has assessment been viewed over time and has this developed and progressed or does it remain fundamentally the same in its key principles?

TRAINING TO TEACH

When I was training to teach I took the one-year PGCE course following my BA in English Literature. Once you had taken out the holiday breaks and the time spent on teaching practice that left only about 30 weeks (or just 180 days!) of university time to tackle all aspects of teaching and learning: a tough job for any Initial Teacher Training course (ITT). Therefore, it is unsurprising that I was not given an in-depth study of the history of education; it was much more about the here and now and what I needed to teach the children in my future classes to enable them to learn. So I have loved the time I have spent researching this chapter. Sometimes I have got frustrated, while at other times have been excited, as I have read of the trailblazers who have come before us.

IN THE BEGINNING

Assessment in its broadest sense has been in existence from the very beginning. Stone Age man would have assessed if their shooting range was close enough to allow them to kill a wolf while remaining uneaten themselves, while Roman gladiators would have made a judgement on how skilled their opponent was and how likely it was they were going to win the fight. Making accurate assessments helps to keep us safe, from deciding if it is safe to cross the road to testing our food to see if it is cooked properly. Patricia Broadfoot states that, 'Passing judgement is a central part of social behaviour,' and that we are probably unaware of the number of judgements that we make (Broadfoot, 1979, p. 12). You would have made one when you looked at the cover of this book!

ASSESSMENT IN EDUCATION

However, assessment in education took that idea of making a judgement, or an assessment, and then using it to decide on the suitability or success of a learner. History tells us that the record for the first written exam took place at Oxford in 1702 (Black, 1998, p. 10). However, the 'test trail' then goes fairly cold until the nineteenth century when the education system that we recognise today really started to emerge.

It is impossible to separate the history of education from the social history of Britain. Before the 1800s, the profession or job that one held was pretty much determined at birth, due to the circumstances of rank, class or gender. If you were a girl then your education only required skills to help you run a household. If as a son your father was a blacksmith or miner then you were almost certainly going to follow that same path. Likewise, if you were the eldest-born son in a wealthy family then a career in the law or politics was likely while younger brothers might join the army or the clergy. Position and positioning was everything. Therefore, schooling was of relatively low importance. It was not going to help you determine and then facilitate your career choice. What is more, a period of residence of studying, such as four years at university, equalled the qualification; it was the quantity of time rather than the quality of learning that was required to endorse you for your future career (Broadfoot, 1979, p. 29).

I am sure that if I visited my GP and they told me not to worry, that they had spent the appropriate number of years at university but they just hadn't undertaken any assessments in that time I would not be feeling confident! So it was that in 1815 the Society of Apothecaries created a Court of Examiners to examine and award licences and register successful candidates to practise as an Apothecary in England and Wales (Broadfoot, 1979, p. 30). This was a key development in the journey of formative summative assessment and other professions started to follow suit. No longer was it okay simply to have completed the course, but there was now a need to prove that you were competent in what you could do. It also promoted competition for jobs. The assessment system as we recognise it today had been born.

A NEW VIEW OF EDUCATION

There was now the option to study your way out of your social position and as a result society became more mobile as a wider range of professions became increasingly available to a wider range of individuals. Education was therefore viewed in a new way. It became something worth considering as now it really had the power to facilitate a change in one's prospects. From 1833, the government even offered grants to enable poorer children to attend school, widening the reach of opportunity further still. Indeed, nearly all children had some degree of schooling at this time. It was the Newcastle Commission of 1861 which put the cat amongst the pigeons when it sought to review the quality of education that was being provided:

> *We have seen overwhelming evidence from Her Majesty's Inspectors, to the effect that not more than one fourth of the children receive a good education. So great a failure in the teaching demanded the closest investigation; and as the result of it we have been obliged to come to the conclusion that the instruction given is commonly both too ambitious and too superficial in its character ... and that it often omits to secure a thorough grounding in the simplest but most essential parts of instruction.*
>
> (Newcastle Report, 1861)

Their solution to improving the quality of education available was to introduce testing with the incentive for teachers being that they would get paid according to pupils' results. No doubt this was viewed as a win-win situation as it would help with relieving the burden of the government budget in supporting schooling for so many children while simultaneously improving standards. However, as Broadfoot comments, this simply led to drilling and rote-learning and frequent testing in the three Rs due to the 'high stake' nature of the tests (Broadfoot, 1996, p. 201). I have to say it feels as though we have made a close return to this with the performance-related pay that is currently finding favour in our present system, where formal summative assessments are perceived to reflect the quality of the teaching. It is also an early indication of the power of tests to restrict the curriculum delivered.

ASSESSMENT AND INSPECTION

Although the first Her Majesty's Inspectors (HMIs) were appointed in 1840, it wasn't until 1899 that the first Board of Education was established. They issued a report in 1911 asking for a review of the role of examinations in their usefulness for preparing school-leavers to go on to employment. However, this was not acted on and instead by 1917 the School Certificate (SC) had been born. As time moved on so too did the expectation placed on achieving end-of-schooling qualifications. Because it was only the grammar schools that could issue the SC, primaries were under greater pressure to ensure that their pupils passed the eleven-plus.

Gipps and Stobart identify the era of the eleven-plus as the 'heyday of the standardised test in primary schools', as schools' success rates were measured by the proportion of pupils going on to grammar schools (Gipps and Stobart, 1993, p. 64). This feels very much like a forerunner to performance tables today, where assessment is used to judge 'success' rather than to review what a child knows.

INTO THE FUTURE

Following the 1944 Education Act, driven by the then Education Minister Richard Butler, all children had been assured a free secondary school place and the chance to gain a qualification, following an increase in the school leaving age to 15. (It would not be until 1972 that this would reach 16.) However, the 1960s and 1970s saw a two-tier education system in place with grammar and private schools each running an alternative education as there were still different qualifications awarded at the end of each route. This eventually changed in 1988 with the arrival of the new GCSE (for the first time, all pupils would be assessed against the same norm-referenced criteria) and the new National Curriculum with its identified key stages for assessment. This is a key moment for us in our whistle-stop tour of the history of assessment for it was at this point that the idea of accountability, reliability and validity of assessments really started to take off. Cue the arrival of: Task Group on Assessment and Testing (TGAT) 1987; 1988 Education Reform Act; Schools Examinations and Assessment Council (SEAC) 1988; Qualification and Curriculum Authority (QCA) created 1997; National Assessment Agency 2004; Ofqual 2008; Standards and Testing Agency (STA) 2011. And so it goes on.

For primary schools, the arrival of the new National Curriculum really was the start of a new era. From 1991, all Year 2 children were assessed at the end of Key Stage 1 with the same hurdles waiting for Year 6 children at the end of Key Stage 2 from 1995. There will be plenty of time throughout this book to discuss the helpfulness, or not, of these particular summative assessments and I shall therefore attempt to avoid getting on my political soapbox too much in the first chapter! However, I feel that I would be sharing the voice of many professionals if I said that the years from 1988 to 2014 were a time of ever-shifting sands. As governments came and went, targets around expected levels of achievement of these assessments continued to change. So too did the format of the tests. I have listed a few key changes below.

- 1990 Key Stage 1 test pilot

- 1991 All Year 2 pupils tested

- 1993 Lord Dearing Review slims down National Curriculum

- 1995 Key Stage 2 tests introduced

- 1996 First primary school/Key Stage 2 performance table published

- 1997 New Labour government sets target of 80 per cent L4+ for Key Stage 2 by 2002

- 2000 Revised National Curriculum

- 2001 New target set of 85 per cent L4+ for Key Stage 2 by 2006

- 2003 Progress measures start to appear on Key Stage 2 performance tables

- 2005 Key Stage 1 external tests are replaced with internal teacher assessment

- 2008 Data for pupils achieving Level 4+ in English AND maths also published

- 2011 Phonics screening pilot

- 2012 First year of phonics screening for all children

- 2013 Introduction of separate Key Stage 2 test for Punctuation, Grammar and Spelling

- 2013 Floor standard that 60 per cent of pupils in a school must get L4+ in reading, writing and maths

- 2014 New National Curriculum

- 2014 Calculator no longer allowed in Key Stage 2 maths test

- 2014 Key Stage 2 Reading test is ramped rather than themed

- 2014 First stage of moving away from assessment through levels

- 2016 First round of testing against the new national standards using an interim framework

These changes are reflected in the 2009 commentary from The Teaching and Learning Programme (TLRP):

If policy changes has been hyperactive, in one sense this is not surprising because assessment has been asked to perform an increasing number of functions in recent years; from judging individual pupils to evaluating schools and monitoring national performance.

(TLRP)

SWIFT CHANGES

For me, the 1990s represent a time of listening to Take That, watching *E.R.* and burning my mouth eating Pop Tarts. Yet in the world of assessment it was the decade that saw the rise of 'Levelling' and then 'Sub-Levelling'. (I need to say here that I gave much thought as to whether these terms required the status of a proper noun and decided that due to the enormity of their impact that they should!) The initial plan from the Department of Education and Science was to just use Levels. These were broad statements that summarised a level of performance, scaling from Level 1 to Level 8 and beyond. However, as the decade progressed, the focus on data as a means to measure pupil, and therefore school, performance increased. So too did the need to demonstrate progress over shorter periods of time rather than just the end of key stages. First there was the need to make a summative judgement at the end of each school year, and then at the end of each term, or even half-term. The breadth of the Level Descriptors was therefore deemed to be insufficient to show progress over shorter periods of time and in 2001 Average Point Scores (APS) arrived to enable further numerical data-crunching to take place with Sub-Levels following hot on their heels.

I think that it is important to state here that at the point that the National Curriculum and Key Stages and Level Descriptors were created in 1988, Sub-Levels were never part of the plan. At no point did any government or education department give explicit guidance to educators as to what a child was required to do to secure, for example, 3a in reading as opposed to 3b, in the same way that they had for whole Levels. The closest they have come to this were the 'recommended' Assessing Pupil Progress grids (APP), linked to the National Strategies in 2008, which gave instruction towards a best fit judgement, or the thresholds given for Key Stage 2 tests which informed teachers if a child's score enabled them to qualify for a 4b or just a 4c. Teachers were therefore left to make their own judgements as to how far along a Level descriptor a particular child had got at a given point in time. Despite in-school moderation, and external moderation around Years 2 and 6, there was still room for personal interpretation as to what constituted these Sub-Levels. This seems incredible given the importance that APS were given in evaluating school performance.

LEAGUE TABLES

School performance became very much a public affair during the 1990s. The first primary league tables were published in 1996. There have been various arguments for why this was a productive move; some have argued that it enabled parents to be fully informed about the choice of where they should send their children to school while others argued that there should be greater accountability for how public money was being spent. There have also been those voices championing the test with public results as the way to drive up standards. However, critics claimed that it created a 'name and shame' culture and, as it was based purely on test scores, was not an accurate indicator of the quality of education provided. Neither did it take into account the context of the school or the starting points of the children. Caroline Gipps states that educational assessment is not high stakes but public test data is (Gipps, 1994, p. 161). League tables remain part of the education landscape today. Some of the concerns stated above have been addressed and progress now carries as much gravitas as attainment, and context of the learners carries more weighting.

However, the publishing of performance tables reinforces the 'high-stake' nature of the end of key stage summative assessments. Coupled with this is the presence of the data analysis produced by the education department and used by those bodies that make external judgements, such as Ofsted. The current format is Raiseonline, produced by the Department for Education. Until 2015, it made rigorous use of APS to track attainment and progress of pupils' performance against national averages. As assessment now moves into the new post-Levels era, the format of this annual data report will need to metamorphose into something new, but its message will, no doubt, continue to carry the same status.

The rise of the Sub-Level also gave rise to the education system's infatuation with 'tracking' and the noughties saw an explosion in paper and computer-based systems for tracking pupil progress. Suddenly children were being coloured-coded into red, amber and green, depending on how close they were to the Sub-Level targets that had been set for them. Schools agonised over how many Sub-Levels were required for 'acceptable' progress over the course of any one academic year. 'Assessment Leader' became a new role, which often meant 'the person who looks at the tracking and spots patterns and identifies children who appear to be falling behind'. Don't get me wrong – the use of tracking data and its analysis can be really helpful for spotting trends and ensuring that children do not get left behind. However, the fixation on tracking can distract us from the process of assessment. You will be able to read more about that in Chapter 3.

However, at the same time as the historical narrative detailed in the pages above was playing out, so too was an alternative one. Remember the 1911 review by the Board of Education? One of their recommendations was to move away from a simple end of phase exam and to look instead at other ways to improve learners' chances as they moved into places of work, such as teachers talking to future employers about pupils' strengths and areas for development (Broadfoot, 1979, p. 33). Then there was the Hadow Report of 1933 which argued against set standards being expected for infant schools: 'In none of this should a uniform standard to be reached by all children be expected. The infant school has no business with uniform standards of attainment' (Swaffield, 2008, p. 10). I think it is also important to mention here too the Plowden Report of 1967 which challenged educators to look at the child as a whole and to centre learning around them. These are examples of past voices who wanted to lead policy down a path away from the dominance of the formal summative assessment.

Added into this are the voices of those outside the government remit who nonetheless sought to affect policy making. The Assessment Reform Group (ARG), formerly known as the Assessment Task Group (ATG), was active from 1989 to 2010. It worked tirelessly to share an alternative view of assessment in the form of formative judgements which impact directly on learning – you will be able to read more about that in later chapters. Paul Black and Dylan Wiliam's key piece from 1990 on formative and summative assessment is now compulsory reading for anyone who is involved in teaching, yet I do not recall *Inside the Black*

Box being on the book list when I was doing my PGCE in 1996/7. How much I missed! Throw into the mix Carol Dweck's pivotal work on growth mindsets and John Hattie's research on what really makes an impact on learning and the stage is set for a battle of minds rather a neat meeting of them.

THE PRESENT DAY

And so we come to the present day. The arrival of the new National Curriculum in 2014 gave the perfect opportunity for a review of the Levels assessment system to see if it remained fit for purpose. The Department for Education stated in May 2013 that as there was to be new curriculum content, a new assessment system needed to be established and consequently Levels would be permanently removed. Tim Oates, who chaired the expert panel that reviewed the National Curriculum between 2010 and 2013, explains the reasons for moving away from Levels. First, there was the concern around the negative affect on children's learning when they used Levels to label themselves, for example as Level 3, and how this had the power to place a ceiling on expectation. In addition to this lay the perceived clash between the unnecessary pace that was driving children though Levels and the core principle of the new National Curriculum of studying fewer key concepts in more detail. He states that teaching and learning should focus more on the breadth and mastery of constructs, rather than the need to move constantly on to the next thing. He also talks about the inconsistencies in the use of Levels, presenting three different ways in which Levels were decided upon. Finally, he explains that the top-performing countries in the world do not use a Levels assessment system (Oates, 2014).

So, from September 2014, teachers of children in Years 1, 3, 4 and 5 embarked on a new assessment journey, with those responsible for Years 2 and 6 joining in a year later. The Department for Education was clear that no guidance would be given to schools as to how they were to replace the old system. It was for schools to decide what was best for them and the needs of their new curriculum and their learners. I have heard Mick Walker, former Executive Director of Education at the QCA and advisor to the NAHT's (National Association of Headteachers) commission on assessment without levels, observe that the teaching profession complains when the government tells them what to do but that equally they moan when they are not told what to do. Some local authorities gave direct instruction or 'recommendation' to their schools while others remained silent, possibly biding their time in case future central instruction was upcoming. This was not the case.

In May 2014, nine schools were awarded the Assessment Innovation Award grants, although this is now only recorded as being eight schools. The aim here was to invest in grass roots projects and to share best practice and resources. My own school, Hiltingbury

Junior School, was the ninth school but as we ultimately did not take the grant money we no longer appear on any of the literature. That was the furthest the Department for Education went in making any recommendations. A Commission on Assessment without Levels met from March to May 2015, publishing a final report in September 2015. Chaired by John McIntosh, the expert panel put forward six key recommendations around how the profession can best support one another moving forward without Levels. However, they made it clear that, 'The report does not provide schools with a template for assessment without levels but offers guidance and support to help schools in designing their own assessment policies, in parallel with their curriculum policies' (McIntosh, 2015, p. 4).

FUTURE OUTLOOK

From 2016, pupils' attainment at the end of Key Stages 1 and 2 is instead to be measured with Scaled Scores. Progress measures will remain in a state of flux until 2020 where the Key Stage 2 Scaled Scores will need to be compared against the old Key Stage 1 Average Point Scores. Throw into this mix the latest Year R baseline assessment and the sands appear to set to shift until at least 2023.

Chapter summary

- The basis of our education and assessment system holds its roots in the social history of this country.

- Formal summative assessments came about as a way to ensure quality of learning and suitability to carry out a profession competently.

- Formal summative assessments have fed notions of selection and competition.

- Assessment has been used over time to hold the performance of schools and teachers to account.

- Formal summative assessment has held the lion's share of authority in school accountability over hundreds of years.

- Although the format of formal summative assessments continues to change, their use for judging school performance remains constant.

- There has been a growing voice to champion the role of formative assessment in our education system.

- The latest assessment system has gone the furthest in fusing summative and formative assessments together.

References

Black, P. (1998) *Testing: Friend or Foe? Theory and Practice of Assessment and Testing.* London: Falmer Press.

Broadfoot, P. (1979) *Assessment, Schools and Society.* London: Methuen.

Broadfoot, P. (1996) *Education, Assessment and Society.* Buckingham: Oxford University Press.

Duke of Newcastle (1861) *The Royal Commission on the State of Popular Education in England* (Newcastle Report). http://www.educationengland.org.uk/history/chapter03.html (Accessed 18.2.16)

Gipps, C. (1994) *Assessment: Beyond Testing: Towards a theory of educational assessment.* London: Falmer Press.

Gipps, C. and Stobart, G. (1993) *Assessment: A teachers' guide to the issues.* London: Hodder and Stoughton.

McIntosh, J. (chair) (2015) *Final Report on the Commission on Assessment Without Levels.* London: Department for Education and Standards and Testing Agency.

Oates, T. (2014) *National Curriculum: Tim Oates on assessment.* Department for Education https://www.youtube.com/watch?v=-q5vrBXFpm0 (Accessed 17.1.16)

Swaffield, S. (ed.) (2008) *Unlocking Assessment: Understanding for reflection and application.* London: Routledge.

Teaching and Learning Research Programme (2009) *Assessment in Schools: Fit for purpose?* London: TLRP.

Further reading

Conner, C. (1991) *Assessment and Testing in the Primary School. Basingstoke*: Falmer Press.

Desforges, C. (1989) *Testing and Assessment*. London: Cassell.

Gipps, C. (ed.) (1992) *Developing Assessment for the National Curriculum*. London: Kogan Page.

Gipps, C. and Murphy, P. (1996) *A Fair Test?* Buckingham: Open University Press.

Gipps, C., Steadman, S., Blackstone, T. and Stierer, B. (1983) *Testing Children: Standardised testing in local education authorities and schools*. London: Heinemann.

Horton, T. (ed.) (1990) *Assessment Debates*. Milton Keynes: Open University Press.

Hursh, D. (2008) *High-stakes Testing and the Decline of Teaching and Learning: The real crisis in education*. Plymouth: Rowman and Littlefield.

Norris, N. (1990) *Understanding Educational Evaluation*. London: Kogan Page.

Pole, C. (1993) *Assessing and Recording Achievement*. Buckingham: Open University Press.

Sattery, D. (1989) *Assessment in Schools*. Oxford: Basil Blackwell.

Sumner, R. (1987) *The Role of Testing in Schools*. Windsor: NFER: Nelson.

2 PRINCIPLES OF GREAT ASSESSMENT

This chapter will:

- review why we need assessment;
- warn against how we can limit it;
- define the difference between summative and formative assessment;
- clarify the role of tests in assessment;
- identify the key ingredients for assessment for learning;
- propose the key considerations for assessment without Levels.

INTRODUCTION

I once read some wise words pointing out that if pupils learned everything that we taught, at the same pace, then there would be no need to assess them. How true this is! If teaching was simply a case of ensuring pupils were exposed to key concepts, both knowledge and skill based, and that they all assimilated these in a uniform way then the profession would be able to puts its feet up and stop working at weekends. However, this is obviously not the case. Learning is a complex process carried out by complex beings living complex lives; it is never going to produce unified results if left to its own devices. This notion is also expressed by Hall and Burke:

> As learners, we make our own sense and build our own connections no matter how brilliant the teacher. We do not simply discover things. Each learner interprets, makes sense of and builds their own unique representation of what was taught because it gets connected to each learner's unique set of prior understandings.
>
> (Hall and Burke, 2003, p. 5)

This is where assessment steps in. It is the vital tool that allows teachers to do their job effectively. Assessment is the essential link between teaching and learning. I would illustrate the impact of an absence of assessment in the following way. It would be like delivering a new academic course through a series of lectures at the start of a new academic year, all of which have been planned and written by the lecturer in the summer holidays. The first lecture expounds a series of points, disseminates key knowledge and references key skills required that the lecturer has decided are important. No interaction takes place with the learners in the room; they leave at the end of the hour. The lecturer has no idea which students, if any, have understood what has been shared or what misconceptions have taken place. The second lecture is then delivered, just as it was planned a couple of months ago. No adaptations have been made to allow for re-explaining areas of confusion, giving further examples to strengthen understanding or to make links with prior knowledge and experiences. The gap between the achievements of the learners starts to grow. Some learners start to get bored as they are being taught concepts that they already know. Others decide not to go back to the third lecture as they are so confused by what has been delivered and presume that they are not 'clever enough' to be there. And so the lectures continue. The only assessment the lecturer initiates is a test at the end of the course to see who has passed. The number to 'fail' will be unnecessarily high as no assessment took place prior to or during the course.

The example above is an extreme one but it is there to illustrate an important point. Assessment is needed to inform effective teaching. Without it, teaching remains a one-way monologue rather than a two-way dialogue. We might as well programme a robot to deliver course and lesson content if interaction is not deemed to be necessary. Assessment is needed to shape the direction of learning, both in real time (during a lesson) and for future times (such as the following lesson) to ensure maximum impact on the learner. The 1988 ATG Report saw assessment at the heart of the process of promoting children's learning, providing a framework in which educational objectives may be set and progress expressed. (DES, 1988, paragraph 3). This was reflected in past Ofsted 'School Inspection Handbooks', which placed assessment as an underlying factor throughout the grade descriptors for outstanding teaching and which promoted assessment in 2015 to the title of the key judgement of 'The quality of teaching, learning and assessment', due to its recognised status.

PINNING ASSESSMENT DOWN

I think that it is useful to turn to the thesaurus and consider synonyms for the term 'assessment'. Words such as evaluate, appraise, judge, rate, analyse, estimate and gauge make an appearance. These all speak to me of assimilating acquired information into an informed conclusion. That is what we should be doing in the classroom, to assimilate information that is available to us, in whatever form it comes, and then use it to make a decision. Should I slow down? Is it time to move on? Has Cassie really grasped this? Is Siddhant ready for something different? How do I need to change the way that I have presented this so more learners will access the concept? Do we need to leave this until tomorrow? Would ten minutes' fresh air help? Why is Charlotte under the table? Should I move Adam away from Tia? How has Mark managed to do that with his pencil? And so on.

Assessment is a complex art form. There is no simple set of rules that can be followed or a single framework that can be applied to a class of learners to ensure guaranteed results. It is not an exact science. I have enjoyed reading Mary Jane Drummond's observations on assessment and would recommend her book *Assessing Children's Learning* to anyone who wants a better understanding of this essential area. She talks of teachers committing themselves daily to a life of 'bewildering complexity and uncertainty' as they seek to look at learning, a task she describes to be a massive undertaking. I find Drummond's viewpoint that assessment is 'essentially provisional, partial, tentative, exploratory and, inevitably, incomplete' (Drummond, 2003, p. 20) to be vastly reassuring. There were so many times in teaching that I got to the end of a lesson or unit of work and felt that I had not truly understood what each child had grasped and what their next steps, and mine, needed to be. If we look at the gauntlet laid down by Black and Wiliam that each teacher should confront the question, 'Do I really know enough about the understanding of my pupils to be able to help each of them?' (Black and Wiliam, 1998, p. 13) then we can see that this is a commonplace difficulty for many in the profession and one that we need to take seriously.

Short of interviewing every child at length on a regular basis, a scenario which is simply not practical, teachers won't ever be certain of having ascertained a complete level of understanding of all areas of children's learning. Instead the three cores principles are that we need to decide what it is that we really need to know, why we need to know it and when we need to know it. Really smart assessment does just this. It is *focused, purposeful* and *timely*.

A LIMITED VIEW OF ASSESSMENT

Perhaps I should not admit this (for a variety of reasons!) but when I first started teaching one of the jobs that I loved doing in the summer holidays was setting up my mark book for the new school year. There was something very satisfying in laying out the pages with the names of my new pupils, creating spaces for spelling and table test results and allowing space to record returned homework that would hopefully be completed in the months to come. However, as I sit here writing this I am struggling to think what I put in my mark book that was really helpful in the process of assessing how well my class were really learning. It was very much a 'mark book' rather than an 'assessment book'. It was what I recognised from my own time in school that teachers did. They set tests and then they recorded the marks and so consequently I had felt confident to do that too.

Looking back to a block teaching practice in my PGCE year, the warning signs of the limited usefulness of the ubiquitous mark book should have been apparent to me. I had been at the school with my Year 4 class for many weeks and had all sorts of 'marks' in my book. However, when it got to the half term that broke up the ten weeks of the teaching practice, I felt a sudden panic (or realisation) that I didn't really know what they could all do, what they had learnt or what they couldn't do. There was nothing in my mark book to help me. I therefore took home 30 maths books, 30 English books, 30 science books and 30 topic books to trawl through over the half term to attempt to find the missing answers.

As my career progressed, I am happy to say that so too did my mark book. Yes, there were still some test scores tracked, more often in a spreadsheet though so the arrival of a new child to the class did not throw out my neat alphabetical list, but I now had my assessment notebook. This came out regularly during lessons and was my personal prompt to remember to make assessments during the lessons. At the start of the school year it was just blank pages. I would then use each page as I saw fit for a lesson or block of learning. I might write the Learning Objective (LO) at the top of the page and the date and just jot down then names of pupils who had or hadn't grasped this. I might pop in the names of those who needed something different for tomorrow. I might write a name and a quote from that learner that I wanted to use at a later date. It was a completely different type of book altogether.

DEFINING SUMMATIVE AND FORMATIVE ASSESSMENT

This shift in my approach marked my personal journey from reliance on summative scores to exploring formative assessment. Assessment geeks will know that these terms appear to have been first used in the late 1960s with further development of the two in the 1980s and 1990s. When leading training with ITT students I differentiate the two simply by stating that formative assessment *informs* decision making and that summative assessment *sums up*. If you don't do anything immediately with your assessment, if it is a summary that gives you as the teacher some information to store away or report then it is summative. However, if whatever assessment you take provides you with information that informs you there and then for an immediate or short-term change then it is formative assessment.

I am always hesitant to split types of assessment techniques into two groups, one formative and one summative, as I feel that it is missing the point. Let us take the notion of a test as an example, or a quiz as I prefer to call them, which are traditionally seen as living in the domain of summative assessment. Imagine a quiz is set by the teacher, covering some key points that have recently been taught, therefore fitting our previous principle of assessment needing to be focused. Imagine for one group of children the teacher has set the quiz at the end of a two-week unit to see how much they have retained and to compare with the other children in a colleague's classroom. For another group of children the teacher has set the same quiz with the same questions but with two lessons left of the unit to go. The quiz scores are returned to the children so that they can decide which focused workshops to join over the next two days before the unit reaches its conclusion. In both cases the principles of purposeful and timely apply. Yet the first setting of the quiz is summative while the second use of the same quiz is formative.

We can also use the example of 'Thumbs Up'. This was one of the early practical examples of formative assessment seen in primary education. Children are asked to show with their thumbs how they are feeling about their learning – are they up, down or a horizontal 'on the fence'? This really needs to be against an explicit LO with clear Success Criteria (SC) where possible to make this at all worthwhile or else it just becomes a 'how am I feeling today' exercise. However, the use of Thumbs Up is only formative if the teacher or the child does something with this moment of self-assessment or else it is simply 'Thumbs Up So What'! If there are children who have their thumbs down after the time of reflection, something different has to happen for them. They either need to be re-grouped, given additional scaffolding or given a new task. That is formative assessment in action – a change is made in real time in response to an assessment. If, however, the teacher sweeps the room to see how many thumbs are up or down and then continues the lesson without making any changes then it is a summative assessment. The same approach, the same question, the same response from children, but one is formative and the other summative. This supports Black's opinion that, 'The formative and summative labels describe two ends of a spectrum of practice in school-based assessment rather than two isolated and completely different functions' (Black, 1998, p. 35).

So, let us set out some helpful key principles around these two approaches to assessment.

Summative	Formative
Comes at the end of learning – a summing up and happens once	Can come at the start, during or end or learning and can happen more than once at any of these points
Has been planned in by the teacher	Can be planned in or it can be responsive
Provides a snapshot in time	Provides part of an ongoing process or cycle
Result is usually shared as score/data	Results can be shared in variety of ways
Pupils have limited involvement in planning this and using the assessment afterwards (one-way process)	Essential that pupils are very much involved in the planning, carrying out and use of these assessments (two-way process)
Used for making comparisons, identifying trends, reporting on performance, tracking progress and target setting and strategic planning	Identifying where a learner is, what they need to do next and helping to make plans to get them there

Table 2.1 Key principles

Although summative assessment has held the lion's share of professional attention for so long it does not make it the evil cousin to formative assessment. It is important to remember that both types of assessment are useful and necessary. These types of assessment are not restricted to education. Take the world of professional sport. As a supporter of Southampton Football Club I am aware of how much use Saints make of both summative and formative data. Before a match there will be the use of statistics from previous games, both of the performance of their own players as well as that of their opposing team. There will be video footage to analyse as well as data produced by player-tracking software, medical statistics and dietary reports.

There will be information gained from the opposing team, reliable or not, from social media and the rumour grapevine. All this is summative data, reported as facts and figures. It becomes formative when the manager uses it to make decisions about who starts the match on the pitch, who is a substitute and who doesn't even make it onto the bench. Further assessments will then continue in real time as the match is in play. Who is playing well, who is looking tired and who looks like they are likely to get booked and miss the next game if they are not careful? Again, all these assessments are summative judgements but once they are acted on, for example leading to a substitution, then they become formative. And so it will continue after the match in an endless cycle of assessment, leading to decisions of future squads, actions in the transfer windows and changes in management.

ACCOUNTABILITY AND NATIONAL TESTING

I think that the high-stakes nature of football management compares itself well to school leadership. Accountability is high and very public. Football league tables and School Performance Tables reveal summative data in its rawest sense – test results. While football fans see changes to the league tables perhaps several times a week, schools' data is revealed on an annual basis. Either way, these are summative assessments, many taken as snapshots in time under test conditions.

Testing remains a controversial issue in education and deserves some of our discussion time. There are those who believe that testing is the most reliable and fair way with which to compare nationally the performance of individuals and groups of pupils. If each child is taking the same test based on the same content or curriculum that all have had access to then the results should be comparable. It is also viewed as relatively inexpensive and time efficient. Yet there are those that see standardised tests as the gatekeepers of the curriculum. A test can only measure what is 'testable'. Therefore, some aspects of the curriculum cannot appear in a test. The argument then follows that if an aspect of the curriculum cannot be tested it becomes in danger of not being taught at all as teachers feel the need to concentrate on those areas that their pupils will be judged on. The curriculum narrows as maths, English and science become the focus as pupils are 'taught to the test'.

The reasoning of teaching to the test is not difficult to understand. Let us return briefly to our football analogy. Careers are made and broken on the back of results. All school leaders, like football managers, are expected to produce 'better than typical' results. But we can't all be at the top of the league every season! John Hattie argues that we have used test data 'to name, shame and blame' (Hattie, 2012, p. 149). There have been too many stories of teachers and school leaders losing their jobs, careers and personal health following the revelation that they have altered test papers as they felt so under pressure to produce the right results. Yes, schools need to be held to account for how they are spending public money and to show that the children in their care are getting a great education. However, this should not be at the expense of the mental health of those involved, including the pupils themselves. It is also limiting to think that the issuing of tests and the sharing of these results is the simple solution to raising standards of education. All it shows is that what is measured is being taught more. I read a great quote from Michael Armstrong while carrying out my research that stated that testing is 'peripheral to assessment' and that it measures 'no more than the shadow of achievement' (Conner, 1991, p. 40). The league tables for Key Stage 2 simply show how well those children can perform in a test at that school rather than how well they have been learning.

Personally, I have no issue with the setting of the tests themselves. As shared earlier, they can be used either summatively or formatively and the internal analysis of the results with my senior leadership team (SLT) can be very informative. Rather, my concern is with the use of them as an assessment tool in high-stakes performance measurement. As a headteacher, the release of the Raiseonline report in the autumn term is not a date I look forward to, especially as I know that this is being monitored by Her Majesty's Inspectors for any sign of vulnerability. This could be that all our children made expected progress from Key Stage 1 to Key Stage 2, but not as many made better than expected progress, potentially leading to the appearance of 'blue' on our Raiseonline report. Again, we can't all be top of the league all the time but one shouldn't feel fearful that you might end up mid-table in the premiership! I will also add at this point that it still seems incredible that at Key Stage 1 we have teacher assessments whereas at Key Stage 2 these are replaced tests. Surely we should be moving to the point where Year 6 teachers and school leaders can be trusted enough to assess their children too?

ASSESSMENT FOR LEARNING

Stepping off my political soapbox, and away from football analogies, I believe that the most effective teaching and learning happens when both teacher and learner are actively involved in understanding what is being learnt, why it is important, what is needed to be achieved and how this can happen in order to be successful. Therefore, any sort of assessment needs to be able to facilitate this, whether it is summative or formative. This returns us neatly to the principles of assessment being focused, purposeful and timely. This is where formative assessment really comes into its own.

Formative assessment is known by a series of titles, including Assessment For Learning (AfL) and Assessment As Learning (AaL). The key point to these labels is that the learner has to play a central role in the process – they become the lead protagonist in their own educational drama. The titles are not Assessment for *Teaching* or Assessment as *Teaching*. The intention is that the information gathered by the assessor, whether this is teacher or pupil, impacts primarily on the learning, although the teaching should naturally be affected too. The ARG defined assessment for learning as 'the process of seeking and interpreting evidence for use by learners and their teachers to decide where the learners are in their learning, where they need to go and how best to get there' (ARG, 2002, p. 2).

Although recipes for anything can be restrictive I would say that great AfL in the classroom needs a few key ingredients:

- A clear Learning Objective (LO).

- Agreed Success Criteria (SC).

- Clear, relevant and timely feedback.

- Time to act on feedback.

When these are all in place then the magic can happen. I don't think it matters what one calls the LO, as long as the equivalent is in place. It could be We are Learning To (WALT), a Learning Intention (LI) or The Purpose of the Lesson. The point is that it ensures that all involved know what they are aiming for. The SC need to be agreed on, shared and understood by all. These might be a checklist, hierarchical or not, or a differentiated set of non-negotiables. They could be the Tricks of the Trade of a chosen genre or a personalised set of targets that are relevant to the learning. The learner needs to be given time to explore, experiment with, attempt, fail or succeed with the LO. The improvement then comes from the productive feedback from the teacher, a peer or themselves, using the SC as the benchmark for success. Then comes the action on that feedback and that is when the improvement really comes. When all of this happens in the classroom it is magic to watch. I have witnessed five year olds agreeing the SC for their gymnastic sequences in PE and then giving each other feedback as to the elements that were missing and what their peers should include as they try and improve their routine. When young learners are taking this process on board at such an early age they are set for life! The ARG also identified ten principles for formative assessment practice, arguing that it should:

1. be part of effective planning;

2. focus on how pupils learn;

3. be central to classroom practice;

4. be a key professional skill;

5. be sensitive and constructive;

6. foster motivation;

7. promote understanding of goals and criteria;

8. help learners know how to improve;

9. develop the capacity for self-assessment;

10. recognise all educational achievement. (ARG, 2002)

This is a good point to return to my 'assessment book' that I shifted towards in my years as a class teacher. It certainly was a marked step towards a more formative way of assessing, but looking at the four ingredients that I have stated are necessary, or the three key principles stated in this chapter or the ten principles from the ARG, the taking of notes was still very much an assessment work in process. Yes, the observations informed my teaching so much more than what was recorded in the 'mark book', but how often was I sharing my observations with my pupils? Yes, written feedback was used as a way to motivate and to guide next steps, but how many verbal opportunities were missed? Yes, it was closely linked to the planning and I had taken time to understand what the LO was and how this would be evidenced at Level 3, Level 4 or Level 5, but did those observations change the shape of that lesson? Did it change pupils' groupings for the next day or only for the next unit of learning? I would love to go back and teach some of my earlier classes with the knowledge that I have now. Hindsight is a wonderful thing!

ASSESSMENT WITHOUT LEVELS

However, we are now at a key moment in the history of primary school assessment where we do have the opportunity to stop and reflect on what best practice is and how we want to proceed with assessment. Professor Shipman states, 'there is a close and necessary relationship between what we choose to assess and what we value most in the education of our children' (Swaffield, 2008, p. 3). With the removal of the Levels system and the arrival of a new curriculum we have the chance to decide what we value most and then decide how we are going to assess it. Schools now 'only' have to report how children have performed against age-related expectations at the end of each year. Other than that, assessment methods and approaches are largely up to the school to decide upon. This includes what to assess, when to assess it, how to assess it and who to share the information with.

The new freedoms from the Department for Education (DfE), first introduced from September 2014, have caused the teaching profession to stop in its tracks. There has been a huge amount of confusion, concern and, in many cases, fear. I will unpick some of this in the following chapters but would say that most of these concerns have come not so much from the idea of assessing what pupils can and can't do in lessons but rather how to present attainment and progress for external validation. By that I mean Ofsted. That has been the biggest concern of all. What will Raiseonline look like? How can I create a new tracking system to replace the APS charts that we used to use that showed term-on-term progress? What should we use instead of Levels and Sub-Levels? I would say that the majority of concerns have focused on tracking, not assessment. Schools have, not surprisingly, focused on the summative side of assessment, as that is where the high-stakes element lies.

At Hiltingbury, we wanted to make sure that we put the learner at the centre of our new assessment system and this is where the premise for our Learning Ladders came from. The idea that we would have a Ladder for each key skill, with the rungs as the key objectives, printed in a child-accessible book, came first. We wanted the pupils to be as involved as possible in achieving rungs, as and when they came. How those rungs, and rung divisions, would produce 'data' was the not primary concern for us and was something that came later. We wanted to create something that would support formative assessment, not just summative. We did not want to simply re-create an APP sheet by another name that sat in a folder in the teacher's cupboard and never made any contact with the children. That seemed like a missed opportunity.

REDEFINING OUR ASSESSMENT VALUES

Revisiting your assessment policy is a great way to see what it is that your school values. Is it a document that sets out a cycle of summative assessments? Does it give guidance on when the Assessment Leader should be collecting and analysing data? Or does it talk about the principles of assessment in your school and what they are aiming to achieve through these? The NAHT commissioned a report on assessment, which was published in February 2014. This very practical resource recommended seven key principles of assessment, notably:

1. Assessment is at the heart of teaching and learning.

   a. Assessment provides evidence to guide teaching and learning.

   b. Assessment provides the opportunity for students to demonstrate and review their progress.

2. Assessment is fair.

   a. Assessment is inclusive of all abilities.

   b. Assessment is free from bias towards factors that are not relevant to what the assessment intends to address.

3. Assessment is honest.

   a. Assessment outcomes are used in ways that minimise undesirable effects.

   b. Assessment outcomes are conveyed in an open, honest and transparent way to assist pupils with their learning.

   c. Assessment judgements are moderated by experienced professionals to ensure their accuracy.

4. Assessment is ambitious.

   a. Assessment places achievement in context against nationally standardised criteria and expected standards.

   b. Assessment embodies, through objective criteria, a pathway of progress and development for every child.

   c. Assessment objectives set high expectations for learners.

5. Assessment is appropriate.

   a. The purpose of any assessment process should be clearly stated.

   b. Conclusions regarding pupil achievement are valid when the assessment method is appropriate (to age, to the task and to the desired feedback information).

   c. Assessment should draw on a wide range of evidence to provide a complete picture of student achievement.

   d. Assessment should demand no more procedures or records than are practically required to allow pupils, their parents and teachers to plan future learning.

5. Assessment is consistent.

   a. Judgements are formed according to common principles.

   b. The results are readily understandable by third parties.

   c. A school's results are capable of comparison with other schools, both locally and nationally.

6. Assessment outcomes provide meaningful and understandable information for:

   a. pupils in developing their learning;

   b. parents in supporting children with their learning;

   c. teachers in planning teaching and learning. Assessment must provide information that justifies the time spent;

   d. school leaders and governors in planning and allocating resources; and

   e. government and agents of government.

7. Assessment feedback should inspire greater effort and a belief that, through hard work and practice, more can be achieved. (NAHT, 2014, p. 8)

They sit well with Michael Tidd's seven questions that he recommends any school should ask about their assessment system:

1. Can it be shared with students?

2. Is it manageable and useful for teachers?

3. Will it identify where students are falling behind soon enough?

4. Will it help shape curriculum and teaching?

5. Will it provide information that can be shared with parents?

6. Will it help to track progress across the key stage?

7. Does it avoid making meaningless sub-divisions? (Tidd, 2014)

With the removal of Levels as the driving force of our assessment system, schools now need to use guidance such as that listed above to make sure that they are really confident about the underpinning principles of where their school is going next with assessment. They need to do some research, play around with some ideas and see what works best for their learners, but also be prepared to make changes along the way. The ultimate aim is that when children reach the end of Year 2 and Year 6 that they are able to meet age-related expectations. How we use assessment along the way to make sure that they get there is up to us as professionals. How exciting!

Chapter summary

- Assessment is essential to enable quality teaching and learning to take place.

- Assessment is complex and messy.

- Assessment needs to be focused, purposeful and timely.

- Formative and summative assessments serve different purposes.

- An assessment tool can be used summatively or formatively.

- Testing can be useful but high-stakes data is not when important decisions are based on that test result.

- Effective formative assessment should make its presence felt in the classroom.

- Assessment policies should reflect what a school values in the education of its children.

References

ARG (2002) Assessment for Learning: Ten Principles http://cdn.aaia.org.uk/content/uploads/2010/06/Assessment-for-Learning-10-principles.pdf (Accessed 18.2.16).

Black, P. (1998) *Testing: Friend or Foe? Theory and Practice of Assessment and Testing*. London: Falmer Press.

Black, P. and Wiliam, D. (1998) *Inside the Black Box*. London: GL Assessment.

Conner, C. (1991) *Assessment and Testing in the Primary School*. Basingstoke: Falmer Press.

Department for Education and Science (1988) *National Curriculum Task Group on Assessment and Testing*. London: HMSO.

Drummond, M.J. (2003) *Assessing Children's Learning*. London: David Fulton Publishers.

Hall. K. and Burke W. (2003) *Making Formative Assessment Work*. Maidenhead: Open University Press.

Hattie, J. (2012) *Visible Learning for Teacher: Maximising impact on learning*. Abingdon: Routledge.

NAHT (2014) *Report of the NAHT Commission on Assessment.* Haywards Heath: NAHT.

Swaffield, S. (ed.) (2008) *Unlocking Assessment: Understanding for reflection and application.* London: Routledge.

Tidd, M. (2014) 7 *Questions you should ask about any new 'post-levels' assessment scheme.* https://michaelt1979.wordpress.com/2014/03/23/7-questions-you-should-ask-about-any-new-post-levels-assessment-scheme/ (Accessed 17.1.16).

Further reading

Black, P. and Broadfoot, P. (1982) *Keeping Track of Teaching: Assessment in the modern classroom.* London: Routledge and Kegan Paul.

Black, P., Harrison, C., Lee, C., Marshall, B. and Wiliam, D. (2002) *Working Inside the Black Box: Assessment for learning in the classroom.* London: King's College.

Black, P., Harrison, C., Lee, C., Marshall, B. and Wiliam, D. (2003) *Assessment for Learning: Putting it into practice.* Maidenhead: Open University Press.

Briggs, M., Woodfield, A., Martin, C. and Swatton, P. (2008) *Assessment for Learning and Teaching in Primary Schools.* Exeter: Learning Matters.

Gardner, J. (ed.) (2006) *Assessment and Learning.* London: SAGE.

PART TWO

THE IMPACT AND OPPORTUNITY OF LIFE AFTER LEVELS

3 THE IMPACT AND OPPORTUNITY OF LIFE AFTER LEVELS FOR SCHOOL PRACTITIONERS

This chapter will:

- reflect how the use of the Levels system helped us to assess children's learning;
- summarise what the removal of Levels has revealed about how we assess children's learning;
- explore what summative assessment can look like without Levels;
- consider what formative assessment can look like without Levels;
- define what breadth and mastery means with assessment without Levels.

WHAT DID LEVELS EVER DO FOR US?

When members of the teaching profession are asked the inevitable question, 'Why do we assess?' they are quick to reply with a number of responses. Up there with the most common replies is that it enables us to see what 'children know' and 'what their gaps are' and therefore facilitates the planning of next steps. There is usually also a comment around identifying any trends or vulnerable groups in the data to help with strategic planning. Without doubt there is always a comment, too, on accountability, whether this is around external auditors, such as Ofsted, or for the use of in-school judgements from governors for staff appraisal.

CONSISTENCY OF EXPECTATIONS

I think that it would be unjust to say that the now-redundant system of using Levels to facilitate assessment was without any usefulness. If we consider those common responses as to why we assess we can see how Levels helped in all those purposes. In Chapter 1 we looked at how the arrival of the National Curriculum and the new key stages marked a turning point in ensuring a higher degree of consistency, and therefore equality, for all learners. All teachers in all schools across the country had a shared set of expectations of what children should be aiming for. This was made clear in the 1987 National Curriculum consultation document which stated, 'Attainment targets will be set for all three core subjects of maths, English and science. These will establish what children should normally be expected to know, understand and be able to do at around the ages of 7, 11, 14 and 16 and will enable the progress of each child to be measured against established national standards' (DES, 1987 p. 9).

A COMMON LANGUAGE

As the Levels were developed to assist with the assessment of the new National Curriculum, they provided teachers with a shared language to describe how far along this journey a child was in regard to meeting age-related expectations. This was a major turning point in education in establishing equality and transparency. Each subject got its own set of Level descriptors, from Level 1 to Level 8, which were for teachers to use to make a best fit judgement at the end of a key stage, having built up their judgement over a period of time. Teachers became very comfortable with this language. This commonality of expression was strengthened further by the extensive availability of standardised resources from key government departments that exemplified work at a certain Level. These materials ensured that in-school and external moderation could be carried out successfully and confidently, securing the use of the language of Levels further. It enabled the easier transition of pupils between schools and key stages – tracking systems aligned and therefore information on achievement could be shared quickly and easily.

SUB-LEVELS AND SMALLER STEPS

Some would argue the arrival of APS in the noughties began to over-complicate things but for the purposes of this part of the chapter we will focus on why Sub-Levels were useful. The original Levels were designed to help make a ball-park judgement at the end of a key stage; the aim was for Level 2 at the end of Key Stage 1, Level 4 at the end of Key Stage 2 and Level 5/6 at the end of Key Stage 3. However, the movement towards tracking at the end of each school year to provide accountability in terms of internal data meant that the whole Levels did not work – there weren't enough Levels for one per year. This meant that the Sub-Levels were created to break down the progress within a Level further. Hence Level 3c, 3b and 3a, etc. were born. Once those Sub-Levels were in operation, the next step was to start to use them at the end of each term. Senior Leaders and Assessment Managers therefore had an agreed format with which to track attainment and progress over smaller time periods and to use to make comparisons and judgements and to inform strategic planning. Many have said that because Sub-Levels enabled even more accurate tracking of pupil progress, it ensured vulnerable pupils did not fall further behind as their need was quickly highlighted.

LEVELS AS A SUMMATIVE ASSESSMENT SYSTEM

Certainly the use of Levels provided classroom practitioners with ample evidence for summative assessment. There were optional tests, for example, that could be completed at the end of each year of Key Stage 2, which would provide a raw score as well as an APS. There were, of course, the end of key stage assessments, which were used for target setting and tracking. Nearly every school in the country had some form of internal tracking, which took termly teacher assessments and used them to create APS data that recorded the progress for students. These numbers were able to create endless graphs and charts to celebrate positive trends and to highlight possible causes for concern.

LEVELS AS A FORMATIVE ASSESSMENT SYSTEM?

Levels were the framework of the assessment system. Therefore, any assessments that were made using them had the power to be formative or summative, as discussed in Chapter 2. Having said that, it is difficult to make formative assessments to inform next steps when a performance descriptor is very broad, as was the case with the whole Levels. Although Sub-Levels were smaller, there were never official descriptors for these, so identifying next steps in learning required a very good working knowledge of the National Curriculum and sound subject knowledge of how children progressed through key areas such as fractions in maths. The APP Frameworks, produced by the National Strategies, did provide further detail to help with identifying smaller steps rather than just using the broader brush strokes of the Level Descriptors. Where these smaller steps were used to communicate between teacher and pupil where the learner was in their understanding, where they needed to get to and how they were going to get there then yes, the Levels could provide the framework for productive formative assessment. If teachers were delivering a maths lesson on fractions and saw that a child could 'recognise and record fractions that are several parts of the whole such as 3/4, 2/5' (Level 3) then they could make a formative assessment that the next step, either then or in the next lesson, could be to look to 'convert mixed numbers to improper fractions and vice versa' (Level 4).

Yet despite the role that Levels could play in formative assessment, their summative use saw the lion's share of all that they did. The original plan was that

> *much of the assessments … will be done by teachers as an integral part of normal classroom work. But at the heart of the assessment process there will be nationally prescribed tests done by all the pupils to supplement the individual teachers' assessments. Teachers will administer and mark these, but their marking and their assessments overall will be externally moderated.*
>
> (DES, 1987, p. 12)

Further to this the recommendation was that

> *for the external assessments at 7, 11 and 14, standard assessment tasks or*
> *SATs be used; these were to be performance style assessments with a range of response*
> *models and styles with practical, oral and written activities in a range of contexts so that*
> *the tasks would have face and validity ... and would not have undesired washback effects*
> *on the curriculum.*
>
> (Gipps and Murphy, 1996, p. 186)

So while the original intention was that assessment against the National Curriculum would be classroom based, the reality of the manageability of this led to the standard National Tests and from there the use of Levels was primarily one of summative use. Coupled with the importance placed on the use of APS data by Ofsted when judging the effectiveness of schools, it is understandable as to why the tracking of summative judgements became something of a national past-time for school leaders.

WHAT HAS THE REMOVAL OF LEVELS SHOWN US?

When the removal of levels was first announced I did go into a state of shock. For those of you who are familiar with the Kübler-Ross curve model that summarises the emotional stages that we go through in times of significant change, I have to admit to having gone through all of them! There was first the shock followed quickly by denial – surely they were going to change their minds. Then came the anger as I thought about how much work this was going to take to create a new way of assessing pupil achievement, without any direct guidance from the DfE. I then moved on to the resignation stage, recognising that this was actually happening and then quickly to the acceptance and the excitement of all that was to come and the opportunities that it would bring. I don't think that there is anything wrong with going through the negative emotions associated to change; it is the length of time and the amount of energy that we spend on each section that is the most important thing. I am now delighted that Levels have gone but it did take me a while. But I don't think it was a bad thing because in the time following the announcement of the change I had to really think about what I felt about assessment, rather than pottering along with a system that we did because we had been told to do it and we had always done it. As Hiltingbury moved away from the Levels approach of assessing, and the more that I spoke to other school leaders, the following things became apparent to me.

AN OVER-RELIANCE ON SUMMATIVE ASSESSMENTS

We were one of those schools who took a termly snapshot, measured in APS, of where each pupil was in reading, writing and maths. This score was recorded on our tracking software and then various members of the SLT, subject leaders and class teachers undertook data analysis. What was fascinating is that although this termly data marker was supposed to be a teacher assessment, it never really was. This is because daily opportunities for formative and summative assessments had not been made the most of throughout the term and records kept accordingly. Therefore, when it came to the termly teacher assessment, pupils were being asked to complete a test, usually one of the older optional papers produced by QCA, and this was being used to generate a mark which in turn was converted to a Sub-Level to go on the tracker. Although teachers would say that this test was 'informing' their teacher assessment, in reality the test score *was* the assessment, particularly when it came to assessing reading. I have always felt that our Early Years colleagues are the masters of on-going teacher assessment and, as we have moved forward with life after Levels, this is something that we have focused upon. Continuing Professional Development (CPD) has explored *how* to assess as well as *what* to assess. Returning to the building blocks of our profession is incredibly refreshing.

AN OVER-RELIANCE ON APS TO DISCUSS ACHIEVEMENT

As with all schools, Hiltingbury has regular Pupil Progress meetings. We are constantly experimenting with the frequency and format of these to ensure that they have the ultimate impact on teaching and learning. At the first meeting in the autumn of 2014, I sat with the class teacher and their head of year and as normal asked them who the focus children were that they were bringing to the table that day. When I asked them why those children, they talked confidently about the number of Sub-Levels they had, or hadn't made, in the previous year or how many Sub-Levels off track they were if they were to make expected progress by the end of the term. We agreed upon the children and then discussed what they needed and put in place a series of actions that would hopefully enable some accelerated progress. What proved to be fascinating was the following meeting. When the class teacher shared that they had completed all the actions, interventions and approaches we had mapped out they were asked if it had made a difference. Had the pupils made progress? This was when they stumbled. They were so used to telling me if that child had yet moved a Sub-Level that they were quite at sea deciding if acceptable progress had been made now the old measure had been removed. It hit me between the eyes that we were so reliant, me included, in summing up progress in terms of APS that we had started to forget to talk naturally about progress in terms of work in books and what the child could now do that they couldn't do before. It had slipped from our daily routine. We have revised how we work these meetings and this is discussed in Chapter 6.

A NEED TO REGAIN OUR PROFESSIONAL SUBJECT KNOWLEDGE

Let us tie together the two points from the preceding paragraphs. It had become clear that we had become over reliant on using end of term summative tests to measure attainment as well as then relying on the language of APS to help communicate rates of progress. As we moved back to really focusing on where a child was in their understanding, and I mean *really* understanding where they were, we discovered that some of our professional subject knowledge had become diluted. How confident were we to unpick what it was *exactly* about rounding numbers that they were struggling with? What was it with their phonics that was preventing them from blending successfully? Could we identify where in their planning of a fair test that they went wrong? It became apparent that we needed to spend more time really assessing the children, and by that I mean talking with them and asking some pre-planned questions, to grasp where the gaps were. Equally, teachers were then saying that once they had got that, they weren't necessarily sure where to take them next, and how. The honesty in our Pupil Progress meetings and staff training sessions was just fantastic. Teachers were reflecting on their own professional knowledge and finding it lacking. This had happened as a result of the removal of Levels. We were being given the chance to go back to basics and the teachers were really excited about this. That is one way that our Learning Ladders have been so useful to teachers. Yes, we know that children's learning is not linear and they certainly don't progress in straight lines. They jump from Ladder to Ladder and from rung to rung. However, it has enabled us as staff to talk about a logical pathway of learning. It has meant that we have had to unpack the National Curriculum and then unpick the learning behind different objectives. It is only by truly understanding what it is that we are teaching that we can be successful in our pursuit of excellence in the classroom. This academic year has seen my talented maths leader, Sharon Pay, released from class to work solely on maths. She uses her time to team teach, support colleagues in planning, lead CPD that delves into maths misconceptions as well as working with pupils. What an impact this has had on staff's subject knowledge and professional development!

We continue to work with our colleagues at Hiltingbury Infant School to agree outcomes for Key Stage 1 and have also worked with Thornden Secondary School to look at Age Related Expectations (ARE) for Year 7. Shepards Down Special School were our partners for the P-Level Ladders.

A NEED TO PRODUCE NEW STANDARDISED MATERIALS TO ENABLE ACCURATE MODERATION

For years now, schools have been provided with a wealth of standardised materials from the DfE to enable teachers to successfully make decisions as to which Level a child was working at.

Despite debate as to whether Level 2 was the same at Key Stage 1 as at Key Stage 2, the theory was that the Level Descriptors acted like a scale and therefore any child at any age could be placed along it to measure their achievement. However, the move away from Levels has meant that this resource has gone.

Post-Levels assessments are focused on agreeing if a child has met AREs. Between 2014 and the time of going to press, the DfE has shared some sample test materials as well as an interim set of Performance Descriptors for the end of Year 2 and end of Year 6. The difference from Levels is that these AREs are to be applied only at the end of these key stages – they are not a scale that can be used at any point in a child's career. Therefore, as a school we needed to decide for ourselves what the end of Year 1, 3, 4, 5 and 7 looked like. This first required the setting of the Ladders and the rungs. We then needed to find samples of work that exemplified these standards. Only once those were in place would we be able to moderate teacher judgements and move towards a secure way of assessing pupils with a new system. This has required a huge amount of time in staff meetings and through teacher release time. Yes, we could have bought in examples but there would have been no ownership and no unpicking of the subject knowledge and thinking behind the exemplars provided to us. Instead, we have produced these ourselves or agreed them where external examples have been found. There is a danger for schools in these pressured times when time is tight to simply buy in a solution and to tell the teachers 'this is what Year 1 looks like'. I would warn against this wherever possible. Get your staff to know the new curriculum inside and out.

WHAT DOES SUMMATIVE ASSESSMENT LOOK LIKE POST-LEVELS?

AGREEING ON ARE

At Hiltingbury, our summative assessments are focused on whether or not pupils are on track to make ARE by the end of the school year. Pupils will either have met the required standard, they will still be working towards it or they will have exceeded it. Within school, we do this for all year groups. This fulfils our obligation to report to parents their child's progress and to ensure that rates of progress within school are steady and that their final year at Key Stage 1 or 2 is not spent trying to make up for lost time.

Our school recognises that a child has made ARE when they complete the vast majority of rungs for their year group across the Ladders for that subject. The rungs were set by looking at the detail that was available from the National Curriculum, the Performance Descriptors when they became available and using professional judgement. The rungs are the key objectives that we feel need to be grasped and understood. There is not a rung for each aspect of the curriculum or the Ladder booklets would go on for pages and pages! Teachers still plan to deliver and cover the National Curriculum and not to cover the ladder rungs. However, it is the rungs that get the majority of attention in terms of assessment throughout the year.

ASSESSING KEY OBJECTIVES

In terms of summative judgements, teachers are constantly making assessments against the rungs and signing these off when they feel a child has mastered something. In our school, mastered means they have 'nailed it'. They have 'got it'. We recognise that children do not always retain all information forever. A colleague from Alphington Primary School in Devon once commented that children are 'temporary custodians of knowledge' and that it takes time and over-learning before they have really acquired something. To this end, one delegate at a conference I was speaking at suggested that we should call our booklets 'Snakes and Ladders' for those times when children appear to have lost the learning! We have overcome this difficulty by stating that if we feel that a child in a few months' time would only need a few minutes as a recap about something before they said, 'Oh yes, I remember!' then that means that they have got it and we could sign that rung off. It would be the same for adults learning something. I remember when I was first taught to use Excel. I had got it and was happy using it. But then I didn't need it for several months and had forgotten that you needed the equals sign at the start of the cell to make a formula work. It only needed a quick reminder and I was away again. It didn't mean that I hadn't nailed it the first time but simply I had been learning other things in between time and so I needed a five-minute refresher.

At Hiltingbury, each rung is divided into three steps. The first two have an equal weighting of 25 per cent but the third carries the weighting of 50 per cent. This is because we believe that a child needs to show that they have grasped something over more than one lesson and in more than one context. We are seriously pursuing the idea that mastery equals achieved expectations. For us, mastery does not mean that you have exceeded the key objective but rather that you have fully understood it. That is where the third step of the Ladder rung comes in. For example, take the Ladder rung from Year 4 – *I can recognise and work out unit fractions of shapes, measures and sets of objects.* For the first two steps of the rung the child might be asked to calculate '1/8 of 40 squares of chocolate' or '1/6 of the length of your ruler'. However, that final step, worth 50 per cent, needs what we call a 'curve ball' question. Therefore the child might be asked to work out how many sheep a farmer has if 1/9 of them equal 17. They need to demonstrate that they have really understood what 1/9 means, inside and out. Only when the teacher or teaching assistant feels that to be the case does the rung get coloured in and dated in the children's book and the objective ticked off on the tracking system.

TIMING OF SUMMATIVE ASSESSMENTS

Summative assessments cannot all happen at the end of term; we need to be signing Ladder rungs off as we go. They need to be happening continually so we make the most of the assessment opportunities awarded to us as teachers. The use of 'prove it' tasks and curve ball questions are now becoming second nature to teachers. They form part of the planning and happen on a daily basis to build up the bank of evidence in terms of highlighted rungs. The end of a term is the time to step back and review all the summative assessments made across the term and to use these to make an informed judgement of where the child currently is. It is not the time to do a test. Teachers need to be secure in what achievement is likely to look like when a child nails either the first two steps on the rung or the third step. Assessment opportunities to capture this need to be designed and planned in. As time goes on, staff continue to build up a bank of standardised assessments and pupil responses that can be used to help make future judgements and be used to moderate decisions. It is vital that these are created in-house or, if they come from an external source such as the excellent resources from the National Centre for Excellence in the Teaching of Mathematics (NCETM), that they are agreed first by our staff rather than taken and accepted without question. Now is the time to ensure that we have ownership of all aspects of assessment in our school.

TO TEST OR NOT TO TEST?

Tests, or quizzes, do play a part in our summative assessment system but the difference is that now they are created by the teachers. They are designed around what the teacher wants to know rather than what the publisher of the test wants to write questions about. Tim Oates has explained that 'teachers need to become experts in assessment' and I completely agree with this (Oates, 2014). Classroom practitioners should be in control of the information that is gathered about their learners. That is why the hurried photocopying of external tests is no longer witnessed at Hiltingbury at Christmas and Easter time. The exception to this remains with the Year 6 teachers in their preparation with the Year 6 pupils for their SATs tests. I would love to be able to say that we don't hand over curriculum time in the spring term to SATs preparation and that we simply administer the tests to the children in May each year without them ever having the word 'SATs' before. The reality of the situation is that we do make sure that they are as prepared as they can be to do their best. However, this does not mean getting children throughout their time as juniors getting 'used to' sitting formal tests ready for Year 6. That is not a reason to set tests for children, although I think it is still a useful excuse, or justification, for many for relying on them as a source of summative assessment.

While some schools have decided to use bought-in tests that give Standardised Scores (SS) to show term-on term-progress, at Hiltingbury, we record an end-of-term summative snapshot of where each child is along their Ladder journey. This is based on looking at the number of rungs they have got per Ladder for each subject and deciding whether or not they are on track to make ARE by the end of the school year. There are a number of methods you can use to track assessments, and it is important to investigate the options and systems best suited to the needs of your school. We have two systems that we work with to track assessment and progress. One involves the use of the descriptors of Working Towards (WT), Working Within (WW), Mastered (MA) and Excelling (EX) to record end of year judgements against ARE as these are the terms that will be used at the end of the year to report to parents and governors. Another method we use to measure progress is through the online version of Learning Ladders that has been developed by the social enterprise company School Explained. They have created an innovative system which is flexible around the school's chosen assessment policy. The online system works hand in hand with the in class pupil booklets and provides comprehensive information regarding a pupil's progress and next steps. This system has given us the data we need to help with strategic planning for the 400 children in our care. Summative tracking will be discussed in further detail in Chapter 6.

WHAT DOES FORMATIVE ASSESSMENT LOOK LIKE POST-LEVELS?

I think that in many respects formative assessment looks very much like it did before, only now it is taken more seriously. I don't wish to spend lots of time here talking about ways to carry out formative assessment (that all happens in Chapter 8); instead, I want to look at how our attitude to formative assessment has changed.

SEIZING THE MOMENTS TO ASSESS

You may recall my earlier comment that our Early Years colleagues are the masters of on-going teacher assessment. Because they are unable to rely on formal summative assessments (i.e. tests) they ensure that they capture assessment evidence at every opportunity. I once heard someone call children the 'creators of evidence'. They are giving us information every hour of every day; we just need to be open to seeing it. I walked into the Year R base of a school I am currently working with and there in the corner was a girl writing on the big white board on the wall. She had drawn a series of shapes and written '2D' above them. I asked her what she was doing and she told me, 'drawing shapes'. When I asked her why she was doing this she explained that they were learning about 2D and 3D shapes. I asked her if she could tell me the difference and she said 3D shapes are solid and 2D shapes are flat. Finally I asked her if she could tell me the names of the shapes that she had drawn on the board. At this point she started to get her 2D and 3D shapes confused (she gave me a mixture of sphere, triangle and cuboid) but they were all names of proper shapes. This brief conversation, lasting only a few minutes, gave me so much information about where this girl was in her learning. It was not planned but it was certainly informative. A colleague of mine was also in the room and had got stuck in to the home corner, which was set up as a café. She got some children busy taking her order and was able to make some quick judgements about their phonics learning from their approach to writing down her order for 'chips' on their pad. With the removal of Levels we have the chance to see children again as 'creators of evidence' and to be clued into the information they are giving us. This is not just for children in the Early Years but across the key stages.

Mary Jane Drummond states that, 'Assessment is part of our daily practice in striving for quality' and that 'effective assessment is a process in which our understanding of children's learning, acquired through observation and reflection, can be used to evaluate and enrich the curriculum we offer' (Drummond, 2003, p. 13). This, for me, is what formative assessment is all about. It has become more valued with the removal of Levels as teachers have had to start making more qualitative judgements.

TEACHER SUBJECT KNOWLEDGE (AGAIN!)

For effective formative assessment to happen, certain things need to be in place. One of these is teachers' subject knowledge.

> *Teachers cannot assess well subject matter they do not understand just as they cannot teach it well. Teachers have to understand the constructs they are assessing (and therefore what sort of tasks to set); they have to know how to get at the pupil's knowledge and understanding (and therefore what sort of questions to ask).*
>
> (Gipps, 1994, p. 160)

For many teachers, the new curriculum and its new challenge on breadth and mastery has brought into focus the requirement for a renewed focus on subject knowledge. We need to know the subjects we are teaching inside and out. The learning has to be slowed down and therefore, like anything happening in slow motion, errors are exposed. I remember our maths leader challenging some teachers to spend a whole week on factor pairs. That was a concept that would normally be covered in two days. There was an initial struggle because the subject knowledge was not there to unpick the learning successfully. And if we can't unpick the learning successfully into much smaller steps, dolly steps, we cannot assess formatively for the next stage of learning.

If we are unsure of what we are teaching we need to ask our colleagues. I am sure that many of us have delivered lessons where we understood what we needed to get the children to *do* but not *why* and certainly not what to do if they didn't get it. I can remember very clearly a lesson

I had planned in my early teaching days involving tossing coins and recording the results. In the end I had to speak to a colleague because I didn't really have a clue why we were doing it. I just knew how to organise the lesson and that they needed to get filled in on the chart. The concepts of probability we were exploring were not secure in my own mind. If that was the case it was unlikely they would become secure in the minds of my class.

QUALITY QUESTIONING

For great formative assessment to take place, the right questions need to be asked. They need to be designed to draw out useful information. I use the word designed as so often teacher questioning is created out of thin air. We are great at thinking on our feet, and need to be able to do so, but really effective questioning needs some pre-thinking. A great way to go about this is to use the many models based around Bloom's taxonomy. You just need to do an internet search for 'Bloom's Taxonomy Questions' and you will find a wealth of useful ways to construct great questions. An internet search on Dylan Wiliam's advice on questioning is equally challenging and informative. Great questioning is about so much more than just ensuring a balance of open and closed questions. There are some practical suggestions for this in Chapter 8.

ENERGY AND EFFORT

I believe really effective formative assessors are super organised and energetic. Let's be honest, teaching children is an unpredictable pastime. You have your fabulous lesson planned out and then they come back in from playtime, with one child distraught as their Match Attax cards have been stolen, Charlotte and Grace having broken up over an argument based on *The X-Factor* and Ben looking as if he is about to vomit in the sink. The skilled assessor has to battle with the demands of the classroom yet still strive for quality teaching and learning to take place, daily. Because they are organised and energetic, in a matter of minutes Ben has been sent to First Aid, the Match Attax cards waved from the teacher's desk where they had been confiscated in the morning and the girls told that *Strictly Come Dancing* is a safer option and to stay on opposite sides of the classroom until lunchtime. All without breaking a sweat! Then the learning continues.

So, super organised because they have thought ahead and are aware of what they need to capture and how they are going to do it. Teaching Assistants are primed. They have copies of the plans or daily notes and have been assigned children to focus on. Those 'prove it' questions have been shared and the expected answers are known. The teacher has their assessment notebook, or equivalent, out and is actively writing in it. They know what expected progress will look like. They have made the time to have the conversations with children and are going to record those observations somewhere or use them to change the direction of the lesson. Pupils are used to the organised routines of the class and know where to go, independently, to get information to keep their learning going.

I have said energetic because effective assessment can be exhausting. You need to become the Sherlock Holmes of learning. It is no use going round the room, dropping in on each table to ask how they are doing and do they want any help. That is rather like a social call. Instead, there should be a forensic diagnosis happening. Are these children where you want them to be and what proof have they given you? The teacher needs to be judge and jury at this point. Has the learning taken place? The more work that you do in terms of asking purposeful questions then the more assessment material that you will get. A great test for a teacher is to ask someone to come in and visit their lesson at a random moment and ask them if they can point out some children who are on track for the intended learning of the lesson and how they know that. If the teacher can do that then some great assessing has taken place. It also means that they knew what it was they should be assessing. Energetic too as you need to be ready to change the direction of the learning based on what you have seen. That takes us back to 'Thumbs Up So What'. Don't ask the question if you are not really interested in the answer. The aim of the teacher is not to be simply 'looking busy' but instead to be actively engaged with the creators of evidence, the children. The evidence gathered might be of the formative type but equally it might end up being summative. It could be planned or it could be spontaneous. The teacher's role is to recognise it and appreciate it and capture it – then use it.

Chapter summary

- Levels did have their usefulness.

- Levels had become more of a summative tool than a formative one.

- The removal of Levels has caused the profession to rethink much of its practice and knowledge.

- There is no longer a national agreement on what Years 1, 3, 4 and 5 should look like beyond any detail given in the National Curriculum.

- Staff subject knowledge needs to be strengthened. If you can't teach it you can't assess it and vice versa.

- Schools need to decide on a new approach to capturing summative data.

- Formative assessment is starting to carry greater importance than before.

References

Department for Education and Science (1987) *The National Curriculum 5–16: A consultation document.* London: HMSO.

Drummond, M.J. (2003) *Assessing Children's Learning.* London: David Fulton Publishers.

Gipps, C. (1994) *Towards a Theory of Educational Assessment.* London: Falmer Press.

Gipps, C. and Murphy, P. (1996) *A Fair Test? Assessment, Achievement and Equity.* Buckingham: Open University Press.

Oates, T. (2014) *National Curriculum: Tim Oates on assessment.* Department for Education https://www.youtube.com/watch?v=-q5vrBXFpm0 (Accessed 17.1.16).

Further reading

Clarke, S. (2001) *Unlocking Formative Assessment.* London: Hodder and Stoughton.

Clarke, S. (2008) *Active Learning Through Formative Assessment.* London: Hodder Education.

Wood, D. (1998) *How Children Think and Learn.* Oxford: Blackwell.

4 THE IMPACT AND OPPORTUNITY OF LIFE AFTER LEVELS FOR PUPILS

This chapter will:

- set out the need for active learners;
- suggest how pupils can learn with purpose;
- promote the power of reflection and self-assessment;
- explore ways to ensure pitch and challenge;
- champion quality feedback.

INTRODUCTION

I have chosen to shape this chapter around the following statement from John Hattie.

> *Visible teaching and learning occurs when learning is the explicit and transparent goal, when it is appropriately challenging, and when the teacher and the student both (in their various ways) seek to ascertain whether and to what degree the challenging goal is attained. Visible teaching and learning occurs where there is deliberate practice aimed at attaining mastery of the goal, when there is feedback given and sought, and where there are active, passionate, and engaging people ... participating in the act of learning.*
>
> (Hattie, 2012, p. 17)

In this chapter I will look at each of the ideas above from my own perspective and explore what they mean for our pupils in a world of assessment without Levels. I will pick up on 'Mastery' in Chapter 5.

ACTIVE LEARNERS

We can place the best teachers in the world in front of a class and they can tap-dance, juggle and generally pull out all the stops to demonstrate, or perform, great teaching. However, unless there is engagement, real engagement, from the pupils then the teaching is wasted. The learning just doesn't happen.

A SHIFT TO BEHAVIOUR FOR LEARNING

Over recent years, the Ofsted inspection frameworks have shown an increasing shift in the description of good and outstanding behaviour from requiring simply well-behaved children to instead expecting behaviour for learning. Consider below the grade descriptors for *The behaviour and safety of pupils in school* from the January 2013 *Ofsted School Inspection Handbook* (p. 40).

Outstanding (1)

- Pupils' attitudes to learning are exemplary.
- Parents, staff and pupils are unreservedly positive about both behaviour and safety.
- Pupils' behaviour outside lessons is almost always impeccable. Pupils' pride in the school is shown by their excellent conduct, manners and punctuality.
- Pupils are fully aware of different forms of bullying, including cyber-bullying and prejudice-based bullying, and actively try to prevent it from occurring. Bullying in all its forms is rare and dealt with highly effectively.
- Skilled and highly consistent behaviour management by all staff makes a strong contribution to an exceptionally positive climate for learning. There are excellent improvements in behaviour over time for individuals or groups with particular behaviour needs.
- All groups of pupils feel safe at school and at alternative provision placements at all times. They understand very clearly what constitutes unsafe situations and are highly aware of how to keep themselves and others safe, including in relation to e-safety.

Good (2)

- Pupils' attitudes to learning are consistently positive and low-level disruption in lessons is uncommon.
- There are few well founded concerns expressed by parents, staff and pupils about behaviour and safety.
- There is a positive ethos in the school, and pupils behave well, attend regularly, have good manners and are punctual to lessons.
- Pupils have a good awareness of different forms of bullying. There are few instances of bullying and these are dealt with effectively by the school.
- Behaviour is managed consistently well. There are marked improvements in behaviour over time for individuals or groups with particular behavioural needs.
- Pupils feel safe at school and at alternative provision placements and understand how to keep themselves safe.

Figure 4.1 2013 Ofsted Grade Descriptions for Behaviour and Safety of Pupils

There is only one bullet point that is specifically targeting attitudes to learning, with an extra reference in the outstanding descriptor alluding to the fact that well-behaved children help to foster a more positive learning environment. Compare those with the descriptors for *Personal Development, Behaviour and Welfare* from the 2015 Ofsted *School Inspection Handbook* (pp. 52–53) and you will see a very different set of criteria.

Outstanding (1)

- Pupils are confident, self-assured learners. Their excellent attitudes to learning have a strong, positive impact on their progress. They are proud of their achievements and of their school.
- Pupils discuss and debate issues in a considered way, showing respect for others' ideas and points of view.
- In secondary schools, high quality, impartial careers guidance helps pupils to make informed choices about which courses suit their academic needs and aspirations. They are prepared for the next stage of their education, employment, self-employment or training.
- Pupils understand how their education equips them with the behaviours and attitudes necessary for success in their next stage of education, training or employment and for their adult life.
- Pupils value their education and rarely miss a day at school. No groups of pupils are disadvantaged by low attendance. The attendance of pupils who have previously had exceptionally high rates of absence is rising quickly towards the national average.
- Pupils' impeccable conduct reflects the school's effective strategies to promote high standards of behaviour. Pupils are self-disciplined. Incidences of low-level disruption are extremely rare.
- For individuals or groups with particular needs, there is sustained improvement in pupils' behaviour. Where standards of behaviour were already excellent, they have been maintained.
- Pupils work hard with the school to prevent all forms of bullying, including online bullying and prejudice-based bullying.
- Staff and pupils deal effectively with the very rare instances of bullying behaviour and/or use of derogatory or aggressive language.
- The school's open culture actively promotes all aspects of pupils' welfare. Pupils are safe and feel safe at all times. They understand how to keep themselves and others safe in different situations and settings. They trust leaders to take rapid and appropriate action to resolve any concern they have.
- Pupils can explain accurately and confidently how to keep themselves healthy. They make informed choices about healthy eating, fitness and their emotional and mental well-being. They have an age-appropriate understanding of healthy relationships and are confident in staying safe abuse and exploitation.
- Pupils have an excellent understanding of how to stay safe online and of the dangers of inappropriate use of mobile technology and social networking sites.
- Pupil's spiritual, moral, social and cultural development equips them to be thoughtful, caring and active citizens in school and in wider society.

Good (2)

- Pupils are confident and self-assured. They take pride in their work, their school and their appearance.
- Pupils' attitudes to all aspects of their learning are consistently positive. These positive attitudes have a good impact on the progress they make.
- Pupils show respect for others' ideas and views.
- In secondary schools, pupils use impartial careers guidance to make choices about the next stage of their education, employment, self-employment or training.
- Pupils are punctual and prepared for lessons. They bring the right equipment and are ready to learn.
- Pupils value their education. Few are absent or persistently absent. No groups of pupils are disadvantaged by low attendance. The attendance of pupils who have previously had exceptionally high rates of absence is showing marked and sustained improvement.
- Pupils conduct themselves well throughout the day, including at lunchtimes.
- The school is an orderly environment. Pupils respond quickly to instructions and requests from staff, allowing lessons to flow smoothly and without interruption. Low-level disruption is rare.
- Pupils' good conduct reflects the school's efforts to promote high standards. There are marked improvements in behaviour for individuals or groups with particular behavioural needs.
- Parents, staff and pupils have no well-founded concerns about personal development, behaviour and welfare.
- Teachers and other adults are quick to tackle the rare use of derogatory or aggressive language and always challenge stereotyping.

(Continued)

Figure 4.2 (Continued)

> - Teachers and other adults promote clear messages about the impact of bullying and prejudiced behaviour on pupils' well-being. Pupils work well with the school to tackle and prevent the rare occurrences of bullying.
> - The school's open culture promotes all aspects of pupils' welfare. Pupils are safe and feel safe. They have opportunities to learn how to keep themselves safe. They enjoy learning about how to stay healthy and about emotional and mental health, safe and positive relationships and how to prevent misuse of technology.
> - Pupil's spiritual, moral, social and cultural development ensures that they are prepared to be reflective about and responsible for their actions as good citizens.

Figure 4.2 2015 Ofsted Grade Descriptors for Personal Development, Behaviour and Welfare

Clearly there is greater detail here across all points but most importantly there is so much more focus on behaviour *for* learning not *of* behaviour. Language around pride, confidence and attitude are evident. Collaborative learning is required. There is the expectation that learners understand why they are in school and are going to make the most of it. It speaks of longer-term goals with careers advice and a desire to succeed. All this adds up to the need for 'active learners'.

Earlier in the noughties, Hiltingbury Juniors could demonstrate that the majority of its pupils were beautifully behaved and a pleasure to teach – yes, I have been told that there were always a few exceptions, but then they all have their moments! However, it can be very easy for teachers to think that a room of quiet and compliant children equals successful teaching. Having done a stint of supply teaching at one point in my career, I have to admit that there were days that I would perceive as having been successful because I had managed behaviour well and so would go home smiling. As professionals, we can sometimes breathe a sigh of relief when no one was under the table or continually tapping their ruler on the desk while calling out. But this is a dangerous trap to fall into. Quiet children do not necessarily equate to learning children. They can be switched off, disengaged and biding time until the next playtime whilst they gaze placidly in the direction of the board.

THE POWER OF A LEARNING COUNCIL

We need to make sure that our children are active learners and that they understand why we want that for them. Hiltingbury has a Learning Council (LC). Zara Chambers leads the group of pupils to spearhead changing attitudes for children's learning across the school. The pupil councillors are ambassadors for active learning in all classes. You might be wondering what this has to do with life after Levels. We knew that whatever assessment system our school was going to go take on would have minimum impact on our children if they remained the passive learners that we recognised many of them to be. Children need to learn how to learn. Robert Fisher talks about thinking or reasoning as 'the fourth "R"', such is its importance (Bowring-Carr and West-Burnham, 1997, p. 93). We were also very much aware of the research findings presented in The Sutton Trust *Teaching and Learning Toolkit* (The Sutton Trust, 2016), which evidences meta-cognition and self-regulation as having a high level of impact on pupil achievement, which is also reflected in Hattie's *Visible Learning* (Hattie, 2009).

Zara has worked with the LC to look to revise our learning 'goals'. After several sessions, the children came up with 'WE CARE About Learning'. We now have six key learning skills which underpin all that we do.

W – Working together

E – Enthusiasm

C – Creativity

A – Ambition

R – Reflection

E – Enquiry

Then came the work of making sure that the children and adults of the school community knew what these meant and what they looked like in the classroom and the world around them. We needed shared definitions. A document was produced that looked at what the skills meant, how a learner thinks and feels when using this skill, what does the opposite end of the spectrum look like for this skill and finally how it can be strengthened. Some of this came from work I had undertaken at my previous school, Halterworth Primary, where we explored active learning under the acronym REACH. This was based on models set out in *Learning Power in Practice* (Deakin Crick, 2006).

We led launch events with pupils, staff and parents. Whole days of curriculum time were given to unpicking the six learning skills. The weekly Friday celebration assembly now sees certificates awarded against WE CARE rather than for a completed task. For example, a child will be rewarded for Reflection in their story writing, having used feedback purposefully, rather than for the story itself. Once a child receives a certificate they also get the matching badge. This is partly to encourage them to want to 'collect them all' but also so they can be seen as an ambassador to their peers. Assumptions such as, 'creativity happens in art and not maths' have been challenged.

End of year reports no longer have an effort grade but instead a reference to how they are doing against the WE CARE skills. We felt that effort is too subjective and was often being judged against behaviour. We want pupils and parents to understand instead where they are in their behaviour for learning. The LC, under the watchful eye of Zara, undertook learning observations. They decided what evidence they would see in classrooms if the learning skills were in action and set off with their clipboards and lanyards. Following their observations of the learners, as opposed to the teachers, they decided what feedback they would give the children in that class. The first time this was done a few teachers had volunteered to facilitate the process. The impact was so powerful that for the following rounds all the teachers wanted the LC in their class! Messages, which perhaps they, as teachers, had been giving, might have fallen on deaf ears but when it came from their peers the class took it on board and ran with it.

Interestingly, our monitoring of these skills showed that it was Enquiry which was being awarded least in assembly and was the skill the children tended to avoid talking about. It came from the history of inactive learning. The idea of asking questions, contributing and getting involved was something that staff really had to work on harder than the other skills. However, hands now go up for question asking rather than simply to respond to a teacher's request for information. The introduction of Dylan Wiliam's lolly stick idea helps to support this (see Chapter 8). Our Wacky Weeks mean that once a term the children get the chance to pick a topic of their own choosing (chocolate seems to be a popular one!) and they can decide what the geography, maths, English and PE might look like. What would they like to find out about that requires some scientific thinking? How can they apply the art skills that they have developed to this new area of knowledge? I think that as teachers we can often ask the children what they would like to find out at the start of a topic, only to then deliver the planning that we produced in the holidays anyway. We need to get them asking the questions and then let them find out the answers. The Wacky Weeks guarantee that this happens.

GROWING A GROWTH MINDSET CULTURE

Running alongside the six learning skills sits the Growth Mindset philosophy of Carol Dweck. We could see that in our well-behaved children there was an acceptance of the status quo of their success as a learner, or their perceived lack of this. They, and in many instances their parents, felt that they had strengths and weaknesses and that was how it was always going to be. I could take up many pages now discussing Dweck's principles of a Growth Mindset but will instead share with you the key messages that we use at Hiltingbury Juniors (Dweck, 2006).

	Fixed Mindset	Growth Mindset
Your belief	Intelligence is fixed and determined at birth	Intelligence can be developed through efforts and learning
Your priority	Look smart, not dumb	Become smarter through learning
You feel smart…	When you're flawless Achieving easy, low-effort successes Outperforming others	When you're learning Engaging fully with new tasks Tackling challenges and making progress
You avoid…	Effort Difficulty Setbacks High-performing peers	Easy, previously mastered tasks

Table 4.1 Dweck's principles of a Growth Mindset

Dweck's book *Mindset* became essential reading for our staff along with complementary texts such as Matthew Syed's *Bounce*. The idea that, as learners, we can achieve greater things with greater effort has really made an impact on approaches to learning in our school. The LC-led Growth Mindset assemblies to their peers, statements of positivity adorning the walls and adding the word 'yet' to the end of sentences has become second nature to the majority of us.

As schools seek to make sense of a new way forward to assess achievement, the opportunity to get children to be actively engaged in this should not be missed. We have been delighted with how the children have taken ownership of their Learning Ladders booklets and how our whole assessment system is built around them. However, this would not have been the case if the ground work had not already been laid to make them active thinkers and learners in the first place.

LEARNING WITH PURPOSE

I am sure that the vast majority of us have endured learning scenarios which we perceived as having little or no point at all. I can remember a course which left me baffled. Thinking that I would be receiving training on how to effectively lead Performance Management in my school, I was somewhat confused by the path that the tutor led us up. There seemed to be no purpose to what we were doing and as a consequence I learnt very little. Unfortunately the training covered two days so I had to return for a second dose. The title of the course had real purpose but unfortunately the content did not.

WHAT IS THE POINT?

We need to ensure that our children see the relevance and importance of what we are doing so they recognise that they are learning with purpose and consequently they commit themselves to it whole-heartedly. By this, I mean they need to see the purpose both for the short term as well as the long term, ensuring they see it as being something worth putting their effort into.

- How does this piece of learning fit into what I can already do?

- How is it building on skills that I already have?

- Is there going to be a real audience at the end of all this effort, rather than a pretend 'real' audience that my teacher has created?

- How is it going to help me with future learning?

- Will this help me to get a job?

- Are there personal skills I am going to gain from this or is it about knowledge and understanding?

- How long am I expected to spend on it?

- What is the point – will I ever need this later in life?

At Hiltingbury Juniors, we try to provide as many purposeful outcomes for learning as possible. For example, our Year 3 pupils do a geography study of the local area. In English they produce leaflets about the neighbourhood and its facilities, which are given to the estate agents to dispense to their customers for people moving into the area. Year 5 have a unit on Brazil and their outcome is producing a carnival for the parents, incorporating their music, dance and art curriculum. They also engage with local supermarkets to discuss their provision of fairtrade coffee. Where there is an explicit purpose to the learning the buy-in is so much more noticeable.

MAKE THE LINKS

We will talk more about the use of LOs later in this chapter but I feel it is important at this point to say that this is one of the key tools that we can have in making sure that our children understand that learning is taking place. 'We Are Learning To (WALT)... in the context of ... so that...' needs to become a regular feature of pupil and teacher dialogue. When that WALT is a transferable skill then the children can see that there is purpose to what they are learning; yes, it works in this context but it could work in other contexts too – it's not a one-hit wonder. For example, 'WALT defend our goal in a team game'. We want learners to think that the skills they are learning in this hockey lesson could also apply in a football, netball or rugby match. If the WALT is 'to defend the goal in hockey' we are limiting their buy-in, especially if they don't really enjoy hockey.

SEEING THE POWER OF EDUCATION

We want our children to get the learning bug and one way to do that is to ensure they see the power of education. Most children will celebrate when the school closes for snow, a power cut or industrial action. The novelty of a change in routine is very attractive. However, the vast majority of pupils would pass on the option of never having to come to school again. Yes, they love the social aspect but they also see the importance that school plays in their future lives. All schools I have worked in have had people from different jobs come in and speak to the children about their professions. This could be the local community police support officer coming in to talk to the Reception children all the way through to a full-blown careers afternoon. There are not many children who believe that their learning will have no part in the job that they might end up doing. Our job is to reinforce this message whenever we can. I heard of one school that had posters of past pupils in the corridors, celebrating the many jobs and careers they had gone on to enjoy and linking this explicitly with what they had learnt there. And for those children who want to be professional footballers? We need to celebrate with them their exciting plans and then talk about the power of having a Plan B in case they get injured.

PURPOSEFUL ASSESSMENT

As we move away from Levels and seek to establish new assessment systems in our schools we have the perfect opportunity to make sure that it puts pupil learning at its heart. Is your school going to simply create a new 'tracking' system that sits whirring away on the computer ready for data analysis and target setting, or is it going to sit in the heart of the classroom with the children understanding the part that it plays in their learning? Will it help them to learn with purpose?

Our assessment system takes the key skills from the National Curriculum and presents them as Ladders. The children then understand that to be a great reader, for example, you must be a Decoder, Comprehender, Reading Detective, etc. We want them to understand that there are different skills involved in reading, not just 'reading' the words on the page. They need to recognise which skill, or Ladder, they are most confident with and which they need to focus on more. They talk to the teacher when they think that they have proved that they should have a sub-rung signed off, rather than the teacher always telling them that this is the case. They need to see how the different Ladders work together and how, for example, the skills of the reader and writer are so closely interlinked. The Language Lover in reading complementing the Word Wonder in writing is a good example.

The children should notice a difference in the teaching and learning in their school as a new assessment system is adopted. If they do not, then it means that all the school has done is switched from one way of tracking attainment and progress to another behind the scenes. Perhaps the Levels have gone but an alternative 'grade' has been introduced. If it has been practice in your school to share those with the children then yes, they will see that there are now different words being used. But has there been a change in the way that they are being taught, in the way that they are learning? If not, then this is a missed opportunity. Reference to the key skills, or Ladders, and the key National Curriculum objectives, or rungs, are now talked about continually in lessons. For example, in Guided Reading, children appreciate what type of question is being asked. Do they need to use their Reading Detective skills to answer that or their knowledge as a Responder? The purpose of what they are being asked to do becomes clear.

LAUNCHING FOR LIFT-OFF

A launch event is a great way to ensure that you have something worth launching. You want to get your learning community excited about what you are now going to be doing and how it will be different and better than what came before. For us, this included an assembly with my Assistant Headteacher, Diana Massa, climbing a ladder. For Diana, her Ladder was around baking. We stressed that we will all climb the Ladders at different speeds and we are not to worry about anyone else's journey up the Ladder. At this point reference was made to Catherine Pollock, our English Leader, who is a wonderful baker and Diana's role model in the cookery department. There was also the discussion that once you get to the top of the Ladder it doesn't mean that there is nowhere else to go (there is always another Ladder or an even taller one!) and also the idea that we are working on more than one Ladder at a time. As one member of staff said afterwards, 'A cheesy assembly but effective!' The key point is that it left no doubt in the children's minds what these Ladders were all about. Pupil interviews over time have confirmed that the children see the purpose of the new assessment system. We hosted a series of open mornings to share our assessment system with colleagues from across the country and part of this involved a tour of lessons and the chance for visitors to just go and chat with the children and ask them what they thought of the Ladders. Everyone I spoke to was really impressed by how much our pupils understood about the Ladders and how it was helping them with their learning. As the headteacher, that gave me the confidence to continue our journey with life after Levels.

REFLECTION AND SELF-ASSESSMENT
GET THE BASICS IN PLACE

Let's start this section with a great reference from Hall and Burke. 'It is particularly important for pupils to understand what counts as quality in their work, and to be able to monitor their own progress towards their goals' (Hall and Burke, 2003, p. 29). Children from the very earliest age are able to take a look at what they have produced and appraise it in some way. This might be in direct comparison to their friend (*mine is rubbish compared to yours* or *mine is better than yours*). It can be in comparison to what they have done before or their own expectations (*I am pleased with that*). It can simply be an emotional reaction (*I enjoyed doing that*). Our role is to take these natural responses and to help develop them.

However, 'Self-monitoring and self-regulation are complex and difficult skills that do not develop quickly or spontaneously. Teachers have responsibility for fostering and cultivating these skills' (Swaffield, 2008, p. 94). Our younger learners, for example, can be beautifully confident about their achievements. When asked to self-assess their work, perhaps against a given criteria, they will be happy to declare that they have managed it all. For other children, even when all the evidence that has been asked for is clearly present, they will still be hesitant to recognise that their challenge has been achieved.

LEARNING OBJECTIVES, WALTS AND SUCCESS CRITERIA

Before we had the Ladders at our school, we were already working on the children's ability to reflect and self-assess. Our WE CARE skills provided us with the rationale for this; the active learners that we were seeking were starting to appear before our eyes. At the same time we were re-visiting how we were using LOs and SC across the school. When I first arrived in 2013, every classroom had some sort of LO and some sort of SC. However, the issue was in the consistency. Now, I am not one for needing everything to be identical in every class in the school. I try to imagine this from a child's point of view and think how bored you would be by the time that you got to Year 6 and you had heard the same thing in every lesson every day. But there are also times when we need to go back and re-visit the basics and make sure that we are all doing the same thing for the same reason. That was the case with us and LOs and SC. The children were getting mixed messages and therefore their own understanding of how these tools were useful had become confused. Monitoring showed the following to be true:

- Not all children knew what LO, LI or WALT stood for in their room.

- They could not explain what they were *learning* but only what they were *doing*.

- They did not all see the link between the SC and the LO.

- They did not all see that the SC would enable them to be 'successful' in achieving their goals.

- They were not involved in setting the LO or SC.

It was one of those times that reminded me that we should presume nothing. Talking to the children and watching them learn provides us with so much evidence as to how well teaching and learning is *really* going in our school.

So, we agreed that we would all use the term WALT but that although it could be written in short-hand in books we needed to keep saying the term in full so that it was clear it was all about what we were learning. There was the expectation that the WALT would be around a transferable skill wherever possible (this can be trickier in maths) with a context and a purpose stated. We had a drive on SC. We made sure that the link between the two was explicit. We got the pupils writing the SC themselves. Rather than just ticking off against a list of SC at the end of a piece of work they had to provide the evidence, either to the teacher or to their Prove-it-Partner. This made it really clear if they had really understood the SC in the first place. There are more details and ideas around this in Chapter 8. However, the key thing is that these foundations needed to be laid if the children were going to be in a knowledgeable position to self-assess and reflect.

I think it is useful here just to raise some of the concerns that there are around the repeated use of LO and SC.

- Starting every lesson in the same way will switch learners off.

- We are giving them too much scaffolding and are spoon-feeding them by giving them the SC. They should be working it out for themselves.

Shirley Clarke discusses this in *Unlocking Formative Assessment*. She shares research from a range of academics who promote the use of LOs. She argues that without them, 'children are merely victim of the teacher's whim' (Clarke, 2001, p. 19).

Some of her arguments for sharing LOs are summarised as follows:

- Children are more focused.

- Children start to demand it.

- Develops a culture of learning.

- Quality of work improves.

- Greater ownership of lesson.

- Automatically self-evaluative.

- Ensures teacher understands the LO.

- Teacher's expectations rise.

- Reinforces relevant vocabulary. (Clarke, 2001, p. 34)

Clearly, there is no need to always start every lesson with them. Getting the lesson going and then asking children what they think the LO is can be really powerful. Clarke argues that the time to share the LO is the point at which they will start to be judged against it (Clarke, 2014, p. 69).

REFLECTION AGAINST THE RUNGS

So, our school now had children who recognised the LO and SC and the importance of each and the relationship between the two. It made the movement across to our new assessment system so much more effective. Each lesson plan has a LO, for the teacher's benefit, which is linked directly to the National Curriculum. That drives the planning. It is presented to the children as the WALT, in child-friendly language. To help with pitch and assessment, the teacher looks at the rungs to see if any of these are relevant – where they are, they are used. Where they are not, then the teacher needs to return to the National Curriculum and our teacher guidance book (for reading and writing).

For the pupils, their role in reflection and self-assessment is based primarily around the rungs. In the early days of the Ladders, teachers were telling children which Ladder and which rung or rungs was/were the focus for that piece of learning. However, pupils were so confident in assessing themselves against the rungs because of the groundwork we had already put in that we were able to move on quickly from this. Teachers can now share the WALT and ask the children to identify which Ladder and rungs will be most appropriate in their learning. Once these are agreed the children decide which ones will be their personal targets, either for that lesson or for that unit of work. We have found some wonderful translucent sticky arrows which the children can move about in the Ladder booklets from lesson to lesson and rung to rung. They are taking ownership of their self-assessment. We encourage them to communicate with their teacher when they feel that they have succeeded on a rung. Although they aren't allowed to sign them off themselves they are able to use their voice to let the teacher know they are ready to be assessed.

Lorna Earl and Steven Katz wrote that, 'All young people need to become their own best self-assessors' (Swaffield, 2008, p. 90). To enable this to happen, the more involvement that they have in the assessment process the better. We have talked briefly of children writing the SC and being involved in the formative side of assessment. That can also be true of summative approaches. They can be the writers of quizzes, or tests, either for other tables in their classes or for the class next door. This requires a really good working knowledge of the LOs and SC that have been used and writing answers demands a clear understanding of expected outcomes. The bonus for teachers is that it creates double assessment evidence.

AVOIDING LABELS

I know that many schools, ours included, have talked Levels when we were getting the children to self-assess. As a Year 6 teacher, I was constantly explaining the SC in terms of what Level 3, 4 or 5 looked like. I remember the year that many schools chose to boycott the Key Stage 2 SATs. A boy in my class asked what it was all about and I explained that many teachers believed I should not have to send my class' work away so that a stranger could tell me that he was a 4c. Bless him, he looked at me and said, 'Well, I could have told them that myself!' At the time it made me smile and I think I was also probably quite pleased that he had a good understanding of where he was on his learning journey. Now, I look back and cringe. He had labelled himself as a 4c because I had.

To help move away from simply re-creating Levels with ARE, we chose to leave the rungs anonymous for the pupils in terms of which year group they related to. They do not say 'I am a Year 3 reader' where once they would have said 'I am a Level 2 reader'. This prevents a glass ceiling limiting expectations and protects children's self-esteem. Instead, they have the understanding that the further up the Ladder you go the more challenging the rung. For most children, this is enough. However, some older children that I have spoken to who have stronger memories of Levels do miss that element of competition and drive. We need to ensure that they get this in other ways.

There is a case, though, I feel, for learners to have some sort of picture, scale or tool which enables them to see that they are moving forwards in some way. If we are constantly told 'well done for that and now you need to do this' we get no real sense of longer-term progression. That is why we chose the Ladders. The image of a ladder was something that we already used in our school to talk about progress in all sorts of things so for us it felt like a natural choice. I have heard people talk about the fact that learning is not linear and that it should not be shown on a ladder. I agree it is not linear and you will have heard several times by now in this book that we expect our children to jump about across Ladders and between rungs. However, I feel that it is imperative that they do feel that they are getting somewhere. There needs to be some sense that a milestone has been achieved, either one set by their teacher or by themselves. Something that Levels did do for many learners was to motivate them to hit that next milestone.

PITCH AND CHALLENGE
MIXED-ATTAINMENT LEARNING

Much of what I wish to say here reflects the practice of Halterworth Primary School where I worked previously. I would also recommend reading *Creating Learning Without Limits* (Swann et al., 2012) to see another school's perspective on assessment without Levels.

It can be too easy to put a glass ceiling on what our children are able to achieve. This is not usually planned and often a result of well-intentioned actions by us as professionals. A story that I often tell comes from a former colleague and her experience on her teaching practice. A teacher she was working with had grouped her class into ability tables and then labelled them from Killer Whale to Plankton. Yes, Plankton. Although this incident often draws grasps from people, I would challenge us to reflect on what is really the difference between that and grouping them from Hexagons to Circles? Or indeed any form of ability grouping? Is not the message we are giving that there is a Plankton table, even if we have called it something clever that doesn't appear to fit within a hierarchy? Our children need to get the message that there is challenge and expectation for all of them in our lessons. With the removal of Levels there is no longer the option to talk about Level 2 work or Level 3 work.

There are now simple things that are part of our practice at Hiltingbury that ensure challenge is available to all our pupils. We do not use them all of the time, but they are common practice. (See Chapter 8 for more details.)

- Current attainment classes and/or groups are very rarely used.

- Usually, tables are of mixed current attainment.

- Children have learning buddies who are relatively close to them in terms of current attainment but not an exact match.

- Children can opt out of some whole class inputs if it is learning they already feel confident with.

- They can opt in and out of carpet clubs for additional teaching as required.

- There are choices of levels of challenge of work that the pupil decides on rather than being directed to by the teacher.

- There is the option to independently mark some of what they have done (particularly in maths) so that they can decide if they are on the correct level of challenge.

THE CHOICE OF CHOOSING

A common question around children choosing their own level of challenge is how we ensure they always select the correct one. The short answer is that we can't. It is part of a longer learning process where the children need to be guided and given helpful feedback on those instances where perhaps they have got it wrong. Indeed, there are some occasions when the teacher will tell pupils what task they need to take on, informed by their assessment of what the learner achieved the day before. However, one argument I have for this question is that I don't believe that teachers themselves always get it right. Let us return to Black and Wiliam's question, 'Do I really know enough about the understanding of my pupils to be able to help each of them?' I don't think that we as teachers can be 100 per cent sure what level of challenge each child should start their learning with. It therefore makes sense to get them involved so it at least becomes a dialogue rather than a dictatorship.

Pupils must be able to make an informed choice, though. It should not come down to a gut feeling of what they fancy having a go at. This takes us back to the importance of the LO and SC. They need to see how the challenges build on each other so that they recognise where they are pitched.

Interestingly, my experience has been that children will tend to go for the safer option when they are first offered choice of challenge. They will rely on their past experiences or knowledge of where they feel they are in relation to their peers to help them make a decision. I was working with a group of Year 5 children who had been given the choice of challenge for the first time. One child said, 'I'm going for the middle challenge because I was in the middle set for maths last year'. There was a glass ceiling on his expectations that had been placed there by the school, due to the way that his learning had previously been organised.

CELEBRATE FAILURE AND GET IN THE LEARNING PIT

There needs to be an explicit culture in a school that tells children that failure is something that is celebrated. Only then will children feel confident to give those harder challenges a go. Dweck observes that pupils may, 'avoid challenging tasks and do not ask questions out of fear of failure – their energies are concentrated on performance goals, not learning goals' (Hall and Burke, 2003, p. 52). The message that it is good to go wrong needs to be shared over and over again so that everybody really believes it. When I talk to our parents I tell them that if by the time their child leaves us they have never failed then we have failed them. We have children who volunteer to come up in celebration assembly and share their failures that week and what they learnt from them. Quotes around failure and resilience are everywhere and you will commonly here the expression, 'Great wrong answer!' I love the image of the 'learning pit'. Internet research suggests this should be attributed to John Edwards and Jim Butler. It turns that negative feeling of 'I don't get it' into 'what am I going to do about it?' We need to be modelling this all the time to the children. When I asked in an assembly once who had seen me getting things wrong all 400 children put their hands up. A colleague at a school I have recently been working with was modelling to the children in their PE lesson and commented to them that she was finding it a bit tricky. In response, a Year 1 pupil started to chant, 'Persevere! Persevere!' That is when you know that they are really grasping the message.

QUALITY FEEDBACK

Quality feedback is a topic that could fill a whole book so I am going to deliberately reduce what I have to say to some concentrated key points. First, I am talking about feedback as opposed to simply marking. At Hiltingbury we replaced our Marking Policy (which was more a set of codes and rules) with a Feedback Policy. This new document ensured that we were clear about what we wanted our feedback to achieve, how it would look and what role the children would have in this process.

We have used the short video clip and matching images known as *Austin's Butterfly* to make sure our children really buy into the power of feedback. If you have not seen it then first watch it yourself and then show it to your class (Expeditionary Learning Schools, 2012). The children are not fazed by the American-style presentation and instead really focus on the growing image of the butterfly. When the last image is presented I have seen children clap, they are so impressed. It is a great tool to use in class to share the power of acting on *quality* feedback.

STAR, STEP, STRATEGY

Harris and Bell assert that, 'Assessment without communication is of doubtful value: communication between the teacher and the learner is an essential part of the learning process and should be on a regular basis' (Harris and Bell, 1990, p. 88). We concur with this and to this end tweaked our policy accordingly. Using the Northern Ireland Curriculum 'Assessment for Learning' resources as our starting point, we shifted from 'Two Stars and a Wish' to 'Star, Step, Strategy' (CCEA, 2016). Yes, the 'wish' had pointed out what they needed to improve on but it gave the learner no help with how they were going to achieve that. So the 'wish' became the 'step' but it was the addition of the 'strategy' that made all the difference. This helped them to plan a way forward to act on the advice. It might be a prompt, an example, a direct instruction of a task to do, a request for expansion. It is never a rhetorical question. As soon as you start with 'Can you...' then the response from the learner is likely to come back as, 'No!' When I talk to children as to which of the three they find most useful they tell me it is the 'strategy' as it tells them how to make their work better. The 'Star, Step, Strategy' also applies to verbal feedback. It acts as a scaffold in the same way so that the learner can clearly recognise that feedback is actually being given and that they need to respond to this.

VALUE FEEDBACK TIME

All schools I visit have a routine for different colour pens for different stages of writing. Ours is currently blue ink or pencil to compose in, green to self-edit and then red to respond to any feedback. I think that the advantage we all find is that we can easily track the impact of any feedback given, both in the short term and in the longer term. We have to make sure that both with responses to feedback and also to the signing off of rungs that our children don't perceive that as 'done and finished with'. We have to ensure they recognise that this is learning that they need to continue to apply over time, rather than seeing it as a discrete exercise. I have deliberately not talked about feedback from teachers but just feedback as this incorporates teaching assistants, peer and self-assessment. Again, this requires time and training but is equally powerful when done well.

For children to recognise the importance of feedback, they need to see that their teachers value it too. This means that quality response time is given on a regular basis. Those teachers who worry that there is so much curriculum to get through that they can't spare the time to 're-visit' the learning from the last session are missing the point. The power of that feedback must be deemed to be as or more important than what is to be taught next. So proper time needs to be assigned for this and clear expectations set so that all children will respond as indicated. It is not an optional exercise.

SUMMATIVE FEEDBACK

As we have moved away from Levels and towards Ladders we are making sure that our feedback provides us with opportunities to harvest further assessment evidence. How learners respond to those 'strategies' is very informative of their level of understanding. Equally, the 'Prove It' questions and tasks that we ask learners to respond to provide a great evidence base. This is most often in maths, where a 'Prove It' question is written. Our children recognise this as a way that they can show the teacher that they have grasped something and that often leads to the signing off of a rung.

So what of giving grades to our learners? Many schools used to either regularly or occasionally give feedback in the form of grades. As we move away from Levels it is the perfect time to consider how purposeful this is. Dylan Wiliam is one of many researchers who has argued that giving grades is counterproductive and that it 'enhances ego rather than task involvement' (Black et al., 2003, p. 46). Data shows those children who receive feedback only rather than those who receive either a grade or a combination of feedback and grade show a faster rate of progress. So the power of feedback top trumps the grade.

However, moving ahead without Levels is producing its own set of problems for our students. As stated earlier, at Hiltingbury we don't share with our children which school year each rung is associated with in the National Curriculum. Instead, we focus on the achievement of rungs. However, in July 2015 we came to the first end-of-academic-year report to send home to parents. As well as the personal comments and curriculum highlights (more detail in Chapter 5) we also reported their attainment against ARE. For a child in Year 3, for example, their report would give the Performance Descriptor for the subject for Year 3 and then whether their child was Working Towards, Working Within, Mastered or Excelling for that end-of-year expectation. That was when I was hit by a curve ball that I had not seen coming. A parent came to see me to let me know how upset their child was that they were 'Working Towards' their year group expectations. The reason they were upset was because they saw that as the 'bottom grade'. With the Levels system, if they were a 3c, they knew that beneath that was a 2a, 2b, 2c and so on. But their perception was that this was not the case for the Working Towards. This is a potential issue for us all, no matter what assessment system we choose.

Chapter summary

- If we want to make the most of this new era of assessment then we have to put pupils at the heart of it.

- If pupils do not notice a difference in teaching, learning and assessment in school then an opportunity has been missed.

- Formative assessment needs to be genuinely valued. It can't be an add-on to a summative tracking system.

References

Black, P., Harrison, C., Lee, C., Marshall, B. and Wiliam, D. (2003) *Assessment for Learning: Putting it into practice.* Maidenhead: Open University Press.

Bowring-Carr, C. and West-Burnham, J. (1997) *Effective Learning in Schools: How to integrate learning and leadership for a successful school.* London: Pearson.

Clarke, S. (2001) *Unlocking Formative Assessment.* London: Hodder and Stoughton.

Clarke, S. (2014) *Outstanding Formative Assessment: Culture and practice.* London: Hodder Education.

Council for the Curriculum, Examinations and Assessment (2016) 'Assessment for Learning' http://ccea.org.uk/curriculum/key_stage_1_2/assessment/assessment_learning (Accessed 24.1.16).

Deakin Crick, R. (2006) *Learning Power in Practice: A guide for teachers.* London: Paul Chapman Publishing.

Dweck, C.S. (2006) *Mindset: How you can fulfil your potential.* London: Constable and Robinson.

Expeditionary Learning Schools (2012) 'Critique and Feedback – the story of Austin's Butterfly'. https://www.youtube.com/watch?v=hqh1MRWZjms (Accessed 24.1.16).

Hall, K. and Burke, W. M. (2003) *Making Formative Assessment Work.* Maidenhead: Open University Press.

Harris, D. and Bell, C. (1990) *Evaluating and Assessing for Learning.* London: Nichols Publishing.

Hattie, J. (2009) *Visible Learning.* Abingdon: Routledge.

Hattie, J. (2012) *Visible Learning for Teachers: Maximising impact on learning.* Abingdon: Routledge.

Ofsted (2013) *School Inspection Handbook.* London: Ofsted.

Ofsted (2015) *School Inspection Handbook.* London: Ofsted.

The Sutton Trust (2016) *Teaching and Learning Toolkit.* https://educationendowmentfoundation.org.uk/toolkit/toolkit-a-z/ (Accessed 24.1.16).

Swaffield, S. (ed.) (2008) *Unlocking Assessment: Understanding for reflection and application.* London: Routledge.

Further reading

Adams, K. (2009) *Behaviour for Learning in the Primary School.* Exeter: Learning Matters.

Boaler, J. (2009) *The Elephant in the Classroom: Helping children learn and love maths.* London: Souvenir Press.

Claxton, G. (2002) *Building Learning Power.* Bristol: TLO.

Claxton, G., Chambers, M., Powell, G. and Lucas, B. (2011) *The Learning Powered School.* Bristol: TLO.

Hallam, S., Ireson, J. and Davies, J. (2002) *Effective Pupil Grouping in the Primary School.* London: David Fulton.

Hansen, A. (ed.) (2012) *Reflective Learning and Teaching in Primary Schools.* London: Learning Matters.

Ireson, J. and Hallam, S. (2001) *Ability Grouping in Education.* London: Paul Chapman.

Swann, M., Peacock, A., Hart, S. and Drummond, M. (2012) *Creating Learning Without Limits.* Maidenhead: Open University Press.

Syed, M. (2010) *Bounce: The myth of talent and the power of practice.* London: Fourth Estate.

5 THE IMPACT AND OPPORTUNITY OF LIFE AFTER LEVELS FOR PARENTS

This chapter will:

- review how parental involvement in schools has changed over time;
- summarise what it is that parents want to know from their child's school;
- examine how the removal of Levels supports a parent's understanding of their child's learning;
- consider the potential challenges posed for schools in reporting to parents without Levels.

A SHORT HISTORY OF PARENTAL INVOLVEMENT IN EDUCATION

The 1997 White Paper, *Excellence in Schools*, stated that, 'Parents are a child's primary educators and our partnership approach will involve them fully' (Secretary of State for Education and Employment, 1997, p. 12). This is now readily accepted in the teaching profession but it was not always the case. When the education system as we know it was being created, the link between school and home was often non-existent. Those children who did go to school might be boarders, disappearing for months at a time to a place their parents might not even have visited. Or perhaps children attending the local school would leave each morning with their siblings, returning for tea with their parents who relied on their own memories of schooling to help inform their ideas of what their children had been doing all day.

It was the 1967 Plowden Report which challenged that status quo as it argued that, 'schools had a duty to encourage parental interest in their child's education and that children's levels of achievement would improve, as they benefitted from positive parental attitudes' (Vincent, 1996, p. 24). As the education system took a more definitive shape and new curriculums were mapped out, further advice was given to schools, and indeed to parents, as to how home–school partnerships should be forged. Sheila Wolfendale comments that from the 1980s onwards, 'increasing attention has been paid to parents' needs and rights to be kept informed about school business as well as their child's progress' (Wolfendale, 1992, p. 71). Partington and Wragg summarise the various Acts of the 1980s, which gave parents more power and influence in how the school system was run (Partington and Wragg, 1989, p. 5:

1980 Act

1. The right to be elected by fellow parents on to school governing bodies.

2. The right to be given information about schools.

3. The right to be consulted over the choice of school.

4. The right to see minutes of governors' meetings.

1981 Act

1. The right to a suitable education for a child with special educational needs.

2. The right to be consulted over the assessment of such needs.

3. The right to see documentation about a child's special educational needs.

1986 Act

1. The right to an annual meeting between parents and school governors.

2. The right to information about the school's financial affairs.

3. The right to appeal if a pupil is excluded from school for more than five days.

1988 Act

1. The right, with sufficient support from other parents, to bring about a ballot to decide whether the school should remain under local authority control.

2. The right to 'open enrolment' (stopping local authorities from putting artificially low limits on schools to even out numbers across schools).

My research led me to numerous books from the 1980s that sought to help schools work through what home–school partnerships could look like. As parents had been kept at arm's length for so long, it was easy to see them at best a nuisance, at worst a threat. The pages are full of ideas that are now common practice across the education system: communicating through newsletters; curriculum information evenings; open days to come and see the school in action; coffee mornings; getting parents to help in class and on trips; ideas for supporting learning at home; parents' evenings and sending home reports. In the 1980s these were modern concepts and many schools were seeking guidance on how to get this new approach to schooling right. It seems incredible to me that my own primary school teachers were the pioneers of something which is second nature in my own practice.

As the education system machine ground on, the importance of the parent in their child's schooling grew. I do not wish to get too bogged down in social politics, but as we moved through the 1990s and the noughties, the notion of the parent as a 'consumer' became more prevalent. Parent choice has led to a greater demand for information from schools to facilitate their decision making. Parents might expect this to be delivered from a distance or to collect it themselves *in situ*, triangulating evidence from a range of sources such as those mentioned in the paragraph above.

And so to the present day. Home–school partnerships are unrecognisable from those 30 years ago. The way that schools communicate with families is multi-faceted and an abundance of information is readily available. This information, for the most part, falls into two categories. First, as general information about the school, such as its vision and aims, day-to-day practical information and how it is performing. Then there is the information that is specific to an individual child. The majority of parents are active and willing participants in their child's education and seek and use the information that they are given. Unfortunately there is not time in this chapter to talk about how to create best practice in home–school partnerships. Instead, this chapter will focus on how life after Levels impacts on the communication of assessment information with parents.

WHAT INFORMATION DO PARENTS WANT FROM SCHOOLS ABOUT THEIR CHILD?

Unless parents are able to get into school to help on a regular basis, their opportunities to gather information about their child are fairly limited. There might be the school run with the chance to grab a quick word with the teacher or perhaps attendance at a class assembly or open day. Children are notoriously difficult to get information out of with regards to what they have been doing in class. A friend of mine asked that well-known question of her son, 'What did you do today?' as he bounded out of Year R and on to the playground at home time, only to be given the answer, 'A poo'. Sometimes less is more! So, other than relying on their child's view of things, the main point of contact to gain information is through school reports and parents' meetings.

The end-of-year report and the short meetings (averaging ten minutes) thus become a vital window into a child's education. So, what is it that parents want to know? My experience has shown it to be the following things:

- Is my child happy and safe?

- Is my child known as an individual?

- Is my child behaving and putting effort into their learning?

- What are the key areas that they are doing well with and what do they need to work on next?

- Are they on track and making progress?

- How are they doing compared to others in the class?

- Are they being challenged?

- How can I help at home?

- How well is the school performing?

Let us now explore these in more detail and see what they mean for parents with the removal of Levels.

IS MY CHILD SAFE AND HAPPY?

Whenever I ask parents what they want to know about their child, the first response is always regarding their safety and happiness. They want to know if they have friends. Have they got someone to play with at break time? Are they being bullied? Are they settled and confident? How often do they smile? Can they cope with the routines of the day? Are they eating their lunch? It is a great reminder that we are focusing on the well-being of individuals, not just statistics. In both the pre- and post-Levels world of assessment, we can too quickly get caught up with academic achievement of children. At Hiltingbury Juniors, we ensure that our initial observations at parents' meetings are personal ones about that child, and that the first thing that the parent reads in the end-of-year report is the personal comment from the child, followed by the equivalent from the teacher. Academic summary comes later. This precedence is reflected in our school values:

- The whole of our learning community will feel safe and happy.

- No child will be invisible at our school.

- We will be an orchestra – we all have a part to play.

- We will be a community of learners.

IS MY CHILD KNOWN AS AN INDIVIDUAL?

I was really challenged by a book that I read, written back in 1969, by Leslie Keating. He challenged his contemporaries with the following:

Can we honestly say we write an individual child's report with that individual, personal, human child in mind? Do we never just write in order to get these blasted reports done? Do we attribute this state of mind to the teachers who wrote the report which our own child brings home from school? What would we think of them if we did?

(Keating, 1969, p. 78)

Now, I appreciate that this book was written a long time ago, just after the Plowden Report was published, but this makes it even more challenging. This man was very much ahead of his time. At a period in history where the information that was shared with parents came in the form of very brief report cards or grades, here he was, championing his colleagues to see their pupils as individuals. Does the teacher today know who in the class is competing in gymnastics at county level or who has read every Michael Morpurgo book, twice? Are the dinosaur enthusiasts recognised as potential future palaeontologists? How many children are there in the class who love science but get frustrated that there are not enough practical experiments? Who was distraught when One Direction announced that they were going to be breaking up? And so it goes on.

Now, clearly as professionals we can't know everything about all our children. If our classes average at 30 pupils and we managed to divide our time equally between them that gives us approximately 11 minutes a day. That is not a lot to cover the National Curriculum along with life, the universe and everything. However, the point is that we need to try. We need to make sure that we take the opportunity to ask those really simple questions, such as, 'What are you getting up to this weekend?' If we seize the moment when we are walking in from our break duty to ask a child what game they were involved in on the playground we can find out all sorts of things. Of course, there is always 'show and tell' (or 'bring and brag' as I have been known to call it) but constructive versions of this can reveal all sorts of interests and passions. Of course, once we know these we can use them to our advantage in their learning. Furthermore, the more connection there is between teacher and pupil the more positive the learning experience will be.

Second, we need to make use of our relationships with parents to help us with this. Julian Stern reminds us that, 'Parents are not cheap substitutes for teachers: teachers are, at best, quite expensive substitutes for parents' (Stern, 2003, p. 71). Yes, some parents can 'pop in' on a daily basis to share a whole host of not-so useful pieces of information, but the majority usually have something genuinely useful to tell us when they arrive at the classroom door. We need to listen to them – really listen to them. By that I mean ask questions and not perceive them as an irritating interruption to our day. Parents can provide us with really useful background information and assessment evidence.

IS MY CHILD BEHAVING AND PUTTING EFFORT INTO THEIR LEARNING?

For many parents, they are reassured to hear that their child is 'well behaved' at school. While joking that, 'they aren't like that at home', you can see the relief in their eyes that this is one less thing for them to be worrying about. Manners and respect are valued by both school and parents so it is important to share concerns about this. Yet as we discussed in Chapter 4, well-behaved children do not necessarily equate to pupils learning at their optimum. Their next question, around levels of effort, takes us a step closer to our learning goal.

As explained in Chapter 4, we have replaced the effort grade in our reports with a reference to how well they were doing against the six WE CARE skills. As well as our concern that assessing effort was very subjective, we wanted to help the children deconstruct what effort in learning meant. What was a good learner? The children have taken to this really well and are now quick to talk about which skills they are strongest in and what they need to do to improve those they are less confident with. There have been some concerns from some parents who felt that effort was potentially the area of their child's report, in the academic section, that they would come out strongly in and therefore did not want to see it removed. Through parent information evenings, we endeavour to show that the WE CARE learning skills reflect effort (Enthusiasm) and more.

To help parents, as well as pupils and staff, have an even greater understanding of the learning skills, the Learning Council are in the process of creating a WE CARE set of Learning Ladders, with one Ladder per skill. The intention is that the school community will be able to see how the learning skills break down into smaller steps and to help them set personal targets accordingly. As with the other Ladders, this will not be a linear journey but will instead structure a possible pathway to enable mastery of these skills. For some children their journey along some Ladders might well differ according to the area of the curriculum in question. This will provide a valuable talking point, both with the parent and the learner.

One of the clearest ways that parents can see their children's involvement in their learning is through parent information evenings. Having taken the idea from the Wroxham School, our spring term meetings for our Year 5 pupils and Year 6 pupils are now led by the pupils. Their presentations initiate a three-way discussion around successes and next steps and is a wonderful opportunity for the parent to really get a feel for how engaged their child is in their learning. When we first decided to try this with Year 6 pupils in 2015, we ran a parent survey and nearly all parents felt it was a positive suggestion; the results afterwards were overwhelmingly encouraging which is why this year we have now included Year 5 pupils. There are some parents who feel that the time would be best spent if they could hear directly from the teacher without the learner there so they can talk about it 'as it really is'. However, the clear pathway of communication with the child at the centre of the discussion, taking ownership of their learning following a period of reflection promotes so many of our WE CARE skills.

WHAT ARE THE KEY AREAS THAT THEY ARE DOING WELL WITH AND WHAT DO THEY NEED TO WORK ON NEXT?

As we move away from Levels, schools have a wonderful opportunity to move away from *presumed* summaries against Sub-Levels and into something more descriptive and purposeful. As professionals, we had started to believe that the use of a Sub-Level gave a clear summary of what a child could and couldn't do. Teachers, for example, might say, 'I'll give that task to my 2as'. The reality was that a child who was a 2a in writing could have very different areas of strength and for development than the 2a writer next to whom they were seated.

It was presumed that parents were also privy to this secret information. Now, there has been much debate around the argument that parents didn't understand Levels. Nearly all parents that I have spoken to have said that they grasped the order in which they went, i.e. 3c came before 3b and that Level 1 came before Level 2. However, the real argument from the commission on the removal of Levels was that parents didn't really know what a 2a meant, just that their child had moved from a 2b to get there and that was a good thing as it showed progress of some sort.

To ensure that parents know where learning is strong and what is a priority for their child, the teacher informs them each term which Ladders are a cause for celebration and which are an area for focus in reading, writing and maths. Although school works to communicate an understanding of the big picture of the key skills to be focused on rather than just on one rung, or key objective, parents can access the detail of their child's attainment of individual rungs. They can do this either by looking at their child's Ladder books in class or by logging onto Ladders at Home.

The online Ladders at Home gives the option of attaching pieces of work that parents can access. This is something we will be exploring as a school; evidence of equivalent set-ups frequently used in Early Years demonstrate how valuable it can be. It is a really clear way of showing parents what their success looks like against a rung. In the same way, as we produce standardisation pieces for ARE, we need to look at sharing this with parents so they have a really strong understanding of what it is that their child is aiming for.

ARE THEY ON TRACK AND MAKING PROGRESS?

Within all the work that I have done exploring assessment after Levels, the issue of measuring progress and ensuring systems of accountability has to be one of the areas that has caused most concern and raised most questions. I will focus more fully on this in Chapters 6 and 7 but here I will touch briefly on this from a parent's perspective.

Where schools were not giving a termly update on progress in Sub-Levels, the impact of moving away from Levels has not been so great for parents. However, for those parents who did understand Levels and who were used to receiving a termly update, there was genuine reassurance around seeing movement from Sub-Level to Sub-Level. For better or worse, the Sub-Levels existed and they provided clear milestone markers that let parents know that movement along the learning journey was being made. Yes, there were some rules that needed to be learnt: a child should make three Sub-Levels progress a year when working within Level 1 and Level 2; if a child was going to make 'expected progress' of APS 12 then they need to make one and a half Sub-Levels' progress a year; a child would not make one Sub-Level of progress per term in Key Stage 2 as they could end up at GCSE level by the time they finished Year 6. However, if parents grasped these idiosyncrasies then they had a basic tool to use to decipher if 'expected' progress was being made and whether or not alarm bells should be ringing.

These Sub-Levels have now gone. Those schools who are now striving to focus on end-of-year reporting against ARE and to use interim communications instead to describe what the learner can do and what they need to work on next, are finding that many of their parents are feeling all at sea. One parent has said that while she can see that the quality of teaching and learning is strong, she feels as if she has to just trust that the end-of-year report confirms that all is well as there are no longer the milestone markers along the way (even if they were flawed). Chapter 6 is the place to go to get all the ins and outs of this issue but this is a good place to point out that it is not always as easy as you think to be idealistic. I can see why so many schools are, I think sadly, going down the route of dividing the year's learning journey towards the end-of-year ARE into three neat stages, or even six stages to represent the half terms, so that they have a new version of the Sub-Levels ready to prove to parents, and others, that progress is occurring. Looking ahead, I can see that as a school we might start to use the language of 'on track for MA ARE at the end of the year', just so that it gives the reassurance that many parents are looking for in the absence of a Sub-Level.

HOW ARE THEY DOING COMPARED TO OTHERS IN THE CLASS?

Theodore Roosevelt once warned that, 'Comparison is the thief of joy'. For many parents, the need to compare starts as soon as their child starts school and concerns around the 'colour' of their child's reading book are often indicative of this. Yes, some parents are competitive, but the majority are insecure and are simply looking for some reassurance that their child is doing ok. Many teachers have said either pre- or post-Levels they would never give a parent their child's position within the class or cohort. Yet when schools have their children streamed into sets or ability groups they are already giving an indication, both to the parent and the pupil, of how they are ranking in the class.

The relevant statistical terms here are *criterion* or *norm* referencing. Criterion-referenced assessment compares performance against a set of criteria as opposed to the performance of others. An example of this would be passing your driving test. In the classroom, this can have the drawback of focusing too much teacher time on 'passing'. Norm-referenced assessment involves ranking learners. Criticism here is that it is elitist, sorting children by hierarchy, and also that it means that there will always be children ranked as low-performing whereas with criterion-referencing there is always the chance that all can succeed. Thank you to Colin Conner for his useful explanation of this! (Conner, 1991, p. 18).

For parents, a ranked (or norm-referenced) position can give a false reassurance. Let me return to a football analogy. A child can be the best footballer in the class, but is that because they actually have the potential to be the next David Beckham (Mr Growth Mindset himself) or because within their class there is no competition? When they move on to secondary school, and are being ranked against a larger cohort, their football prowess suddenly puts them at a lower point in the ranking order and they don't even make the school team. So, what parents need to be asking instead is how their child is doing against national expectations rather than compared to the class. That will give a much better indication if it is likely their child will end up playing in the Premiership!

Life after Levels gives parents a clear indication as to how they are doing against ARE for their school year. At Hiltingbury, end-of-year attainment levels are summarised as WT ARE, WW ARE, MA ARE or EXC ARE. Parents will get further ranking information from the Key Stage 2 assessments. At the time of writing this, the first set of assessments against the new National Curriculum have yet to be taken and there is only an interim set of procedures in place. However, it has been suggested that parents might be given a Scaled Score (SS) to represent their child's attainment in maths, reading and grammar, with writing remaining as a teacher assessment against the descriptors. The SS of 100 will represent what is deemed to be typical for a Year 6 child and then there will be scores that range either side of this. This should follow a normal distribution curve. There has been an on-going debate as to where the 100 SS should sit. Is it to be in the centre of the curve or will it be slightly to the left or the right? We are yet to find out. However, in terms of information for parents, it will provide the ultimate ranking tool. If their child's score is above 100 then they have performed better than the expected level and if the score is lower than 100 then they have not done as well. The further from 100 the score is then the greater the gap from the expected level of attainment. Schools have not yet been given prescriptive guidance as to the format that reporting to parents will take, for either Key Stage 1 and Key Stage 2. As the 100 mark is due to shift slightly each year, the label of scaled score rather than standardised score is the correct term.

ARE THEY BEING CHALLENGED?

When my husband Simon and I owned an independent bookshop, I used to love being in the children's section. I loved story times, chatting with readers and recommending titles, often to parents and grandparents. Now, if I could have had the proverbial pound for every time a relative asked for a book for a child who was 'very bright' then I could have bought out Waterstones. In schools, we are also used to family members telling us how bright their child is and that they need to be pushed, challenged, stretched and extended to make sure that they fulfil their potential. Now, I have no issue at all with ensuring that *all* learners in my care are made to think, puzzle and struggle. That is what makes us all great learners. Instead, what I want to unpick here is what life after Levels means for parents who are concerned about levels of challenge in school.

First, we need to communicate the increased expectations of the new National Curriculum. Everything has ramped up. For many years now I have been part of the expert panel for the Test Review Group for Key Stage 2 reading tests. Over this period of time I have seen the tests move from themed packs to ramped texts and now to a test that encapsulates those old Level 6 elements. The National Curriculum objectives, the recently released Performance Descriptors and moderation materials for Key Stages 1 and 2 clarify that children now need to show higher levels of competencies than ever before. Therefore, MA ARE now reflects a higher level of attainment than it did a year ago. We need to ensure that parents understand this. If their child was EXC ARE a year ago on the old system, for example working within Level 4 at the end of Year 5, then they might find it a struggle that now in Year 6 that is 'only' MA6. Yes, they are still being challenged, it is just with a different measuring tool.

Second, I want to discuss the term 'mastery' which has really come into its own over the last couple of years. It seems to have crept in, ninja style, and everyone is talking about it but with no real unified idea of its definition. Its origins lie with our eastern colleagues. Like so many messages given to education professionals in this country, it is based on the idea that another nation is doing it better than us. This time the focus is on Shanghai. Roy Blatchford, in his report for the *Guardian*, prophesied that, 'Differentiation is out. Mastery is in' (Blatchford, 2015). He goes on to explain that the approach comes from 'the teacher's unshakeable belief that all children are capable of learning anything if that learning is presented in the right way'. There is a basic premise that all children are all taught the same thing and that there is a mentality of 'keep up not catch up'. Therefore there is no need to differentiate as every learner can achieve the same thing.

There is much about the idea of mastery that I love, including the raised level of expectation for all pupils. However, there are some issues that are yet to be resolved about how it is being used in our education system. For example, there is still no clear and agreed definition being used between professionals. Some talk of mastery as we do at Hiltingbury, equating to having achieved, mastered or nailed a concept, i.e. meeting the expected standard for ARE. Yet others talk of mastery as moving beyond what is expected and equating to EXC.

Furthermore, there are some muddling messages from the DfE around challenge and higher attaining pupils, who remain a focus group in Ofsted inspections under the label 'most able pupils' (Ofsted, 2015, p. 21). On the one hand, there is the expectation that schools slow down their teaching to facilitate true mastery, supporting the idea of less being more and giving children the opportunity to explore a concept in greater detail for a longer period of time so that they really understand it inside and out. Coupled with this is the idea that rather than rushing on to the next thing, pupils should not automatically be accessing the curriculum for the year group above them but should fully explore the curriculum content relevant to their academic year before moving on. This is a message that few of us as professionals would want to argue with. Yet at the same time we are being pushed to set challenging targets for high numbers of pupils achieving a standard beyond ARE. These are mixed messages and we can't follow two models at the same time.

While these issues are not agreed nationally, it can be very difficult in the current climate to give clear messages to parents around schools' approaches to challenge for children. In this post-Levels world, are we supposed to be advocating pushing their child on to work beyond their ARE or to spend longer than they would have done previously to explore and play with key principles? This is a difficult concept for parents to grasp – it sounds as if their child is being held back in some way and sacrificed for the greater good while other children catch up. This is partly because they are used to seeing the speed at which their child might previously have been 'ticking things off' and associating that with success. It is also due to the perception of their child. Children saying they are bored because they are being retaught something they did the previous year can trigger genuine concern for parents.

Therefore, individual schools need to make the most of the opportunities presented by the flexibility from the DfE to decide on their own stance on mastery and then make sure that it is communicated to the parent body confidently, comprehensively and regularly. We need to ensure that parents understand how the slower approach and the exploration around key objectives provides the sorts of learner that our colleagues teaching GCSEs, A-Levels and under- and post-graduate degrees are looking for. This is the same with other teaching approaches that parents might question when they are concerned that their child is not being challenged. This includes a move away from setting and ability groupings, as well as the use of peer-to-peer support. That is when wider professional reading is essential, research evidence needs to be accessed and used confidently and agreed methods are tightly monitored.

HOW CAN I HELP AT HOME?

Here are some really powerful statistics from School Explained to get us started on this section:

- Parental improvement can improve results of 5–11-year-old children by up to 30%.

- Family participation in education is twice as predictive of student academic success as socioeconomic status.

- Students with involved parents have fewer behaviour problems. (School Explained, 2016)

Parental involvement is not something that we want to dismiss. Therefore, if parents are asking us as schools for ways that they can help at home we need to seize this with both hands and make the most of it.

Now we are without Levels, we talk to our parents at Hiltingbury in terms of the Ladder their child is focusing on for reading, writing and maths. We do this rather than giving a very specific small step, or rung, because children can achieve these targets at varying rates and the reality is that no sooner have you communicated this to the parent then you need to get back in touch to let them know that this has been achieved and that now they have moved on to something else. Instead, we give them the skill that is the priority for developing over time and then give them the tools to help support this. For example, we have a guide for developing questioning in reading that we give to our parents. For each Ladder there is a bank of question openers – which could apply to any book – that the parents can use as a scaffold for asking questions when they are hearing their children read.

One of the most powerful tools that we have as a school to support our parents in supporting their children is Ladders At Home, the online version of Learning Ladders. As well as enabling parents to log on to see how well their child is doing against the rungs, the web-based tool has a link from each rung to specific support and advice about how to help with this at home. This has been created by School Explained and is an amazing resource. For each rung in reading, writing and maths it addresses the following:

- What this means.
- Why it's important.
- How it's taught in school.
- Typical homework tasks.
- How parents can help their children.
- Teacher tips.
- Home activities and games.
- Support activities.
- Next steps.
- Suggested resources.

Parents can take their time exploring the rungs around the relevant Ladder to get a good understanding of what it all means.

We have had so many parent information evenings and in-school events at Hiltingbury that I have joked that we should offer loyalty cards to our parents; they can collect a stamp each time they come and then get a free gift! However, if we really believe that we are co-educators with our pupils' families then we need to provide as many opportunities as we can to work with them purposefully. Atkin and Bastiani observed that,

> *Schools that wish to develop more effective relationships with parents have to communicate not only to parents but with them as well. They have to give information but they also need to take steps to enable parents to express their view points, ask questions and make comments, in other words they have to create a situation in which dialogue between listeners can take place.*
>
> (Atkin and Bastiani, 1988, p. 125)

Our information evenings range from the teaching of spelling to Growth Mindset and e-safety. The important thing is to try and make these a dialogue rather than a lecture. Giving out evaluations at the end of these evenings can be a nerve-wracking activity. However, what it has taught me is that nine times out of ten the area that the parents would have valued more time on is how they can help their children at home. We try now to deliberately expand this section of an information meeting or to incorporate this all the way through.

Then there is homework. Yes, it is one of those areas that will divide parents, rather like Goldilocks trying porridge. There will always be too much or too little and not much that is just right. But whatever a school's homework policy, one thing we need to consider is how we empower parents to support their child with this. We need to consider if the instructions are clear and if certain methods (such as for maths) or areas of subject knowledge are required then we have provided them. One parent has suggested that for maths and English homework we make a link to the Ladder the task supports. This way they can start to see how the different curriculum areas all fit together and how they look in practice.

HOW WELL IS THE SCHOOL PERFORMING?

Paul Black comments that, 'Schools have a responsibility to the public who fund them. One aspect of the discharge of this responsibility is to provide evidence that they are indeed promoting the learning of their pupils (Black, 1998, p. 31). Parents are certainly interested parties of 'the public'. The choice of school is often a huge decision, involving many hours in the initial research and then on-going monitoring to ensure the school's performance has not dipped.

As previously stated, the primary concern for many parents is that their child is happy, safe and known. Therefore, evidence that the school is performing well in these areas will be largely qualitative in nature and might come from a range of sources such as visits into school, evidence from the website and feedback from their own child. For some parents, the fact that their child goes to school happily each day is all that they need to know. This will be unchanged in a post-Levels world.

However, there will always be a natural focus on the academic achievements of a school. These are some of the ways that we communicate with our Hiltingbury parents as to the school's performance:

- Sharing outcomes from Ofsted reports.

- Sharing key outcomes from our annual visit from the local authority.

- Having a clear 'Performance' page on the school website with links to all official government websites that summarise school performance.

- Sharing key data in each school prospectus, as it gets updated.

- Sharing key data to potential Year 3 parents when they come to visit the school.

- Having a weekly newsletter which gives a detailed picture of all that is going on in school in relation to the curriculum.

- Summarising relevant performance information at parent information evenings.

None of this will change in after Levels. However, we will need to make sure that the new measures are explained fully to parents as the national picture changes. For example, the percentage of children who are expected to achieve the new floor standards, either for attainment or progress, looks set to drop significantly. The fact that the DfE altered the floor standard from 85 per cent achieving ARE in reading, writing and maths to 65 per cent is indicative of this. This year's national data is certainly going to be interesting! Parents need to understand this new picture and how their child's school fits into this.

As professionals, we know that our performance is deemed only to be as strong as the data from our last cohort. This can be a blessing if your data has just shot up due to a really strong cohort. It can also be problematic when there is a perceived dip, due to a cohort who perhaps had lower levels of prior attainment and more complex needs. We can be quick to tell the school community that this was a 'weak cohort', but we must remember that there are real children and families behind the performance data. Therefore, it is vital that we show the value all of the data that we have available to us. This can come in the form of sharing how strong teaching is, how rigorous the curriculum is and how robust the assessment system is. That way, when there is a dip parents will presume that it is a dip rather than a downward trend.

Interestingly, while parents want to see that Key Stage 1 or Key Stage 2 data shows consistent standards, there are a growing number of parents who are concerned about the pressure that their own child is under when it comes to the end of key stage assessments and would rather schools did not prepare them in any way but instead just let them sit them on the day and see how they do. This has been heightened over the years as many secondary schools no longer use the Key Stage 2 results as a way to stream pupils as they join Year 7, which was often a strong incentive for parents to ensure that their child did well at the end of Year 6. This would only work if every school in the country took the same approach. It therefore becomes an impossible balancing act, with parents wanting the school's performance to improve while not recognising the high-stakes nature of the assessments. The reality is that even where schools ensure that the quality of teaching and learning is of the highest standard possible, so that by the time its pupils come to key assessment points the pupils are as secure as they can be in their learning and therefore as little time as possible needs to be dedicated to 'getting them ready', there will always be other schools who are ploughing large amounts of time and money into booster provision for children.

Chapter summary

- Parental involvement in their child's education has never been greater.

- Different parents prioritise different information from their child's school.

- The removal of Levels means parents need to learn and understand a new assessment language.

- Schools need to communicate clearly around changes in expectation.

References

Atkin, J. and Bastiani, J. (1988) *Listening to Parents: An approach to the improvement of home-school relations.* London: Croom Helm.

Black, P. (1998) *Testing: Friend or foe?* London: Falmer Press.

Blatchford, R. (2015) *Differentiation is out. Mastery is the new classroom buzzword.* The *Guardian* http://www.theguardian.com/teacher-network/2015/oct/01/mastery-differentiation-new-classroom-buzzword (Accessed 17.2.16).

Conner, C. (1991) *Assessing and Testing in the Primary School.* Basingstoke: Falmer Press.

Keating, L. (1969) *The School Report.* Havant: Kenneth Mason.

Ofsted (2015) *School Inspection Handbook.* London: Ofsted.

Partington, J. and Wragg, T. (1989) *Schools and Parents.* London: Cassell.

Secretary of State for Education and Employment (1997) *Excellence in Schools.* London: Crown Copyright.

Stern, J. (2003) *Involving Parents.* London: Continuum.

Vincent, C. (1996) *Parents and Teachers: Power and participation.* London: Falmer.

Wolfendale, S. (1992) *Empowering Parents and Teachers: Working for children.* London: Cassell.

Further reading

Bastiani, J. (ed.) (1988) *Parents and Teachers 2: From policy to practice.* Windsor: NFER-Nelson.

Cheminais, R. (2011) *Family Partnership Working: A guide for education practitioners.* London: SAGE.

Crozier, G. (2000) *Parents and Schools: Partners or protagonists?* London: Trentham.

Goacher, B. and Reid, M.I. (1983) *School Reports to Parents.* Windsor: NFER-Nelson.

Hughes, M., Wikeley, F. and Nash, T. (1994) *Parents and Their Children's Schools.* Oxford: Blackwell.

Jowett, S. and Baginsky, M. (1991) *Building Bridges: Parental involvement in schools.* Windsor: NFER-Nelson.

Merttens, R., Newland, A. and Webb, S. (1996) *Learning in Tandem: Involving parents in their children's education.* Leamington Spa: Scholastic.

School Explained (2016) 'Learning Ladders at Home'. http://www.laddersathome.co.uk

PART THREE

PERFORMANCE AND ACCOUNTABILITY

6 THE ACCOUNTABILITY QUESTION

This chapter will:

- summarise the challenges around accountability created by the removal of Levels;
- suggest some simple approaches to measuring attainment and progress without Levels;
- suggest how schools can work with Ofsted in a post-Levels world;
- explore how school governors can hold the school to account.

SO, WHAT'S THE PROBLEM?

Over the past couple of years, whenever I have spoken about the theory behind the Learning Ladders, how they are a class-based tool that facilitates pupil involvement in the assessment of their learning, supports planning, supports teacher assessment and reporting to parents, there has usually been a pause and then I am asked the questions, 'So what about tracking? What will it look like for Ofsted?' Although I have often found this frustrating, I do understand the infatuation that we have with tracking. For so long now, data has become a huge part of what we do simply because it has become a huge part of how we are judged. For some of us, our relationship with data had become stronger than it is with the children.

The use of APS made number crunching relatively simple, making the tracking of both attainment and progress possible. Colleagues could use the numerical values to compare the achievement of pupils. Year-on-year achievement could be compared, as could performance in different subjects and different classes or cohorts. Because the point scores were numerical, it was very easy to compare not just end-of-year results but also termly results as it just needed division by three. The possibilities seemed endless.

The removal of Levels, and with it APS, caused the teaching profession to wobble with regards to accountability. How would the broader brush strokes of the end-of-year Performance Descriptors support the degree of intricate detail of data analysis that had been happening with Levels? How would proof be provided that children were making good progress within the year? There has been a particular concern around the 'size' of some descriptors. For example, WT ARE can cover a larger spread of attainment than MA ARE. Consequently, some schools have wanted to break down ARE into smaller chunks of a more equal size so they are easier to measure against. Compounding these concerns has been the lack of information from the DfE as to how progress across key stages would be measured in the years to come. As professionals, we no longer knew what expected progress looked like or how it would be measured.

Another complexity comes from the fact that we have now moved away from a continuous scale of assessment, with Levels, to performance descriptions stating where a child should be in their learning at a given point in time. With the continuous scale, it was possible to attempt to map out the learning journey, giving an estimated arrival time along with likely time intervals for the milestone markers along the way. Now this is replaced with a set of end-of-year expectations. Yes, it is clear where they should be by the end of the year. However, how far along the road to mastering this level of performance should a child be during the course of the year? Is it the case that one-third of the curriculum will be taught and assessed for ARE per term, so in our case 33 per cent of rungs will be signed off? Or is the expectation that teachers can only make judgements against ARE at the end of the year once all the curriculum has been taught in sufficient depth? If the latter is the case, how can termly assessments be made? Finally, where pupils are moving from achieving ARE to achieving ARE at the end of each academic year, there is clear indication of expected progress. However, what about those children who are WT ARE each year, or EXC ARE? How clearly can their progress be seen and is it clear whether the gap to achieving ARE has grown bigger or smaller? Schools can fall into the reassuring trap of simply setting termly tests to use scores as evidence of progress to overcome these issues.

Finally, I think that it is also worth mentioning here that there are some additional complications for accountability due to the differing approaches adopted by differing schools. While the autonomy, and supposed trust, being given to schools is laudable, it can make it harder to carry out external moderation with colleagues, therefore weakening confidence in the reliability of teacher assessments. Furthermore, while schools with low mobility can receive a new child mid-year and swiftly 're-brand' them quite easily, others with high rates of mobility could end up with a weakened system with which to show progress within their school.

SOME BUILDING BLOCKS FOR MOVING AHEAD

I know that I have spoken many times so far about Life after Levels being an opportunity for schools to review what we do. The issue of assessment for accountability's sake is no exception. This is the chance to review what information we want to know that we will find useful in securing quality teaching and learning. Below are some key areas for consideration.

TEACHERS KNOW THEIR CHILDREN BETTER THAN A COMPUTER TRACKING SYSTEM DOES

If a good teacher is asked about any child in their class, they will be able to say if they are a cause for concern, if they are doing well or if they are flying. They don't need to get a spreadsheet out to confirm if the pupil's name is highlighted in green or red. They will be able to explain how they are tailoring their teaching to support or challenge them as well as any barriers to learning that they are trying to remove. As the year goes on, they will get a feel for whether or not they are going to reach MA ARE by July. 'A feel for' is another term for professional judgement. It takes into account all the formative and summative assessments that have been made, both qualitative and quantitative, and creates that sense of whether or not they are on track. As long as all those assessments that have been made are accurate then this 'feel' in December, April or May is valid and therefore useful.

A CLASS-BASED TRACKING SYSTEM CAN BE REALLY SIMPLE

Using the information that teachers can provide as outlined above, really simple tracking sheets can be created that can then facilitate meaningful conversations in Pupil Progress meetings, as well as feeding into whole school data pictures. Below is an adaptation of a grid used by Catherine Redgrave from the local authority assessment team in Hampshire. It can take those teacher judgements from any point in the year to create an indication of how many children in a class are on track for making ARE. The headings are correct for the Hiltingbury assessment model but can be adapted accordingly. This one is set up for December. I would suggest that October is the earliest this could be started as it takes time for teachers to start to build up their field of assessments. Obviously, as the months progress then the more accurate the judgement becomes as the bank of assessments increases.

Year 5 – Class X December Assessments – Reading			
On track for WT ARE	On track for WW ARE	On track for MA ARE	On track for EXC ARE
Sarah	Siobhan	Bethany	Simon
Jonah	Daniel	Simeon	
Carmel	Tamon	Isaac	
	Charlie	George	
	Jake	Joel	
	Charis	Aimee	
	Evie	Shay	
	Olivia		
	Esther		
	Nate		
	Decha		

Table 6.1 Simple Key Stage 2 class tracking sheet

The children in the column who are currently on track for achieving WW ARE against the Year 5 National Curriculum or WT ARE would appear at first glance to be the children to focus on. However, by adding their Key Stage 1 scores then the focus might well shift. (Currently these are set as Sub-Levels but this will change in the years to come.)

Year 5 – Class X				
December Assessments – Reading				
KS1 result	On track for WT ARE	On track for WW ARE	On track for MA ARE	On track for EXC ARE
W	Sarah	Siobhan Daniel		
L1	Jonah	Tamon Charlie	George	
L2c	Carmel	Jake Charis Evie	Bethany	
L2b		Olivia Esther	Simeon	
L2a		Nate	Isaac Joel	
L3		Decha	Aimee Shay	Simon

Table 6.2 Simple Key Stage 2 class tracking sheet with Key Stage 1 starting points

Carmel would appear to be a priority as she gained 2c at Key Stage 1. It would therefore seem likely that she would be able to be WW5 by the end of the year. Olivia, Esther, Nate and Decha look to be a concern as 2b$^+$ children would be expected to get to MA5 yet they are only on track for WW5. While it would appear that George and Bethany have done well, Aimee and Shay should possibly be in the EXC5 column. This of course depends if they were teacher assessed at the end of Year 2 as a 3c or a 3a. Certainly, the addition of the Key Stage 1 results only raises questions, rather than providing answers, as is the case with all data. However, this is a really handy sheet for a teacher to have slipped in their planning file. It has children's names on it, rather than just a set of percentages or numbers. It can be tweaked again by highlighting any key vulnerable groups that the school is focusing on. When the teacher reassesses these children, for example in March, evidence of progress can come in the form of how many children have been moved across to the next column. The changing position of the learners' names over the course of the year provides a clear set of evidence for progress.

An alternative grid suitable for a Key Stage 1 class is suggested below.

Year 1 – Class X				
December Assessments – Reading				
End of Year R result	On track for WT ARE	On track for WW ARE	On track for MA ARE	On track for EXC ARE
Emerging				
Expected				
Exceeding				

Table 6.3 Simple Key Stage 1 class tracking sheet

DISCUSSIONS AROUND PUPIL PROGRESS ARE THE MOST POWERFUL FORM OF ACCOUNTABILITY

Let us continue with the set of Year 5 data created in the section above. The most effective use of this summative data is guiding a Pupil Progress meeting. I don't think that there is a school in the country that does not have some sort of system for the class teacher to sit and meet with a senior member of staff to talk through priority children and set a series of learning targets. Some schools do this termly while others do this half-termly. It might be on a 1-2-1 basis or it might be in a team. It might be part of CPD, for example in a staff meeting, or it might come from release time out of class. Whatever the format, it is the opportunity to talk about children, consider any questions raised by the summative data and plan a way ahead. It is time to pause and plan.

It is helpful for the member of SLT to look with the teacher at any patterns. For example, in their class is it WT children who tend to move, the WW or the MA? Are children moving more in maths, reading or writing? Do any of the vulnerable group children move? What about those that were a focus from previous Pupil Progress meetings? Too often, schools have handed over all assessment analysis to their Assessment Leader and class teachers have been removed of all responsibility, and ownership. All staff need to see in black and white the picture of the data they are responsible for. This is using progress data for accountability at grass roots level.

The discussion then needs to lead on to the teacher's concerns. In other words, who are the children who are keeping them awake at night? Who is baffling them? Who appears to have invisible barriers to learning? The power of talking time here is huge. The size of the school, cohort or class might place a limiting factor on how much time is available but I would always say the more the better. A skilled coach will naturally establish a reflective angle to this discussion. This is a good time to identify more general issues where some changes or modifications in approach to whole class teaching could impact positively on a large number of children.

It is then time to look at some individual children. I would always advocate selecting a few children to really drill into their learning. It can be overwhelming if teachers are asked to focus intensely on all children and the result can end up being diluted. The suggested pro forma below is also based on the work of the Hampshire assessment team. The names of the children would come from the grid above, along with additional knowledge that the teacher has about them. The skill is not so much in selecting the children but in filling out the rest of the grid. It comes back to subject knowledge. The teacher really needs to know what the very next step, or dolly step, is that is required to enable progress to happen and how that will be addressed *by the teacher*. It can be very easy to refer to 'an extra group' run by a member of support staff to provide a solution. What is it that the child actually needs to enable them to be successful? It is perhaps helpful to have access here to the subject leader who can step in as the expert and support and challenge in this area. However it is done, it is imperative that there is a clear intended outcome to measure success against at the next Pupil Progress meeting.

Pupil Progress Meeting December Class X – Reading				
Pupil Name	Specific Next Step	Actions	Intended and Actual Outcomes	On track for ARE?

Table 6.4 Simple Pupil Progress meeting target sheet

In terms of accountability, the Pupil Progress meeting gives the opportunity for a senior member of staff to work with the class teacher to hold them to account in terms of the expectations that they have for the children in their class and the quality and impact of their provision. The two Hampshire-based pro formas give the senior member of staff plenty of opportunity to explore with the class teacher the rates of progress for those children and to understand what the assessment picture for a class or cohort looks like.

A SCHOOL-BASED TRACKING SYSTEM CAN BE REALLY SIMPLE

In a very small school, the approach described above could be all the data tracking that is required, especially when there are small numbers of pupils in vulnerable groups.

But when there are larger groups of children involved, something else can be useful in helping to identify trends. We are lucky that we have the Scorecard system that has been developed for Learning Ladders online. This gives each year's set of rungs, for example in reading for Year 2, a possible score of 100. If a child achieves all those rungs over the course of the year then they are awarded the 100 points. As they move through their time in school their attainment and progress can therefore be tracked in the same way as it was with APS. Each term when we update achievement against the rungs the scorecard automatically calibrates pupils' scores as well as running reports to compare pupils, specific groups and cohorts, such as the Gap Analysis feature. As with APS, the opportunities for data analysis are endless.

But how can schools track summative assessments in a basic way that will stand up to questions of accountability from school governors, the local authority or Ofsted? Something that we established early on at Hiltingbury while the online version was being developed was a simple grid that captured where children were along their learning journey. It recorded the termly summative assessments of their current attainment. The first version that we created was as follows:

Year 5 – Class X					
Termly Summary against ARE					
Name	Vulnerable Groups?	End of previous Year	December	April	July
Hannah	PP	WW4	WT5	WW5	WW5
Sim		WT4	WT5	WT5	WT5
Jordan		MA4	WW5	WW5	MA5
Maggie	SEND	WT4	WT5	WT5	WT5
Arjun	EAL	EXC4	EXC5	EXC5	EXC5

Table 6.5 Simple school tracking sheet against ARE

For children such as Hannah and Jordan, this method felt like a very neat summary. However, when it comes to Sim and Maggie, it is more problematic. How could it be argued that their progress was as strong as Hannah and Jordan's? What the term WT tells us about Sim is that he is not close to making ARE; what it doesn't tell us is how big the gap is and whether it is closing or not. This is also the case with Arjun, although with mastery in mind this would be quite an exceptional case! However adapting this format and referring to WW or MA in relation to a specific year group offers a greater insight into pupil progress.

Year 5 – Class X							
Termly Summary against ARE							
Name	Vulnerable Groups?	End of previous Year	December	April	July	Made expected progress?
Hannah	PP	WW4	MA4	WW5	WW5	yes
Sim		MA3	WW4	WW4	MA4	Yes
Jordan		MA4	WW5	WW5	MA5	Yes
Maggie	SEND	MA3	MA3	WW4	WW4	no
Arjun	EAL	WW5	WW5	MA5	WW6	yes

Table 6.6 Simple school tracking sheet against WW and MA for specific year group

Using the above example, MA to MA between two year groups, or WW to WW between two year groups is expected progress. Therefore, Sim and Jordan have both made the same amount of progress. I appreciate some could argue that having a continuous scale and ARE have replaced Levels but using this at the end of term only and focusing your assessment conversations around the curriculum and next steps is crucial. There should be no references in school to any child as 'a WW4' etc. Should schools want to they could start with WW1, giving that a score of 1, MA 1 with a score of 2, WW2 a score of 3 and so on and then track attainment and progress using those values. That is a similar approach to the one recommended by the NAHT's suggested approach to assessment (NAHT, 2014). Whichever approach you choose it should always help develop staff's understanding of what expectations look like outside their own year group, specifically during the process of standardisation and moderation, as they are getting to grips with the new curriculum expectations. Knowing where your pupils are 'now' is crucial as well as understanding or predicting where pupils may be at the end-of-year finishing point against ARE for their year group.

IF YOU WANT EVIDENCE OF PROGRESS THEN LOOK IN THE BOOKS

Earlier in this book I talked about children being the best assessors of their learning. Recently a young man was sent along to my office to share his work with me and in particular his progress with his writing. He was delighted to reveal, with a great deal of drama, his 'before' and 'after' page. It was a magical moment as he proudly told me that, 'On this page it is just random letters but now it makes sense!' What a wonderful piece of evidence of progress and how it is valued in school.

Clearly, we can't take along every child's book to a governors' meeting to talk about progress or go through them all with an Ofsted inspector. However, schools need to be smart about getting some case studies together to show progress in this way. By this, I mean for each class get the teacher to pick out a few children who are making great progress and keep a portfolio of their work. Get those 'before' and 'after' pieces into a file and be ready to show them off and discuss them. Have them labelled so that anyone who is looking at them knows exactly what it is they are showing. Equally, subject leaders can get progress portfolios up and running to show development in key skills across their subject. The history leader, for example, can do this to show how learners' skills are developing in their use of sources of evidence, both within a school year and over time.

At this point it is important that we come back to subject knowledge, though. Teachers need to be really confident what it is that they are looking for when it comes to showing progress. Can they pinpoint the turning point when the learning took off or a concept was finally grasped? Is there evidence that certain feedback or prompts are no longer required because the learner is now doing that skill independently whereas before it had required scaffolding? Good teachers will be able to leap on this evidence quickly as they were aware of it at the time through their assessments and had planned for it. Developing teachers will need help with this. The use of sandwich learning (do, teach, do) can help to establish this way of thinking, focusing on the difference between 'before' and 'after'. Many schools do a 'cold write' as a way of tackling this. This is followed by the teaching and then a 'hot write' at a later date. That makes it crystal clear where progress has taken place. Equally, whole staff CPD scrutinising books for evidence of progress will be a valuable exercise, particularly where the lead member of staff has carefully selected a range of books to reflect varying degrees of progress. Even more helpful can be prepared questions or tasks that go with these books to scaffold the learning for some staff. For example, 'Find evidence that Harry's understanding of place value is stronger in June than it was in January.'

THE TROUBLE WITH TARGET SETTING

The older I get the more I question what is expected of our profession. I don't mean I am becoming a cynic, only that with greater experience I am in a better position to query our approaches to teaching, learning and assessment. Target setting is one of those things. We are frequently asked to set targets, either for individuals, classes or cohorts. These can be for the end of term, the end of the year or the end of a key stage. Recently this has felt like a numbers game. Partly this is because we are still trying to get to grips with the new National Curriculum and the content of the new statutory tests; it is very hard to predict if Gabe is going to make ARE for Year 6 writing when you have only just been given the moderation materials and the deadlines and expectations around this change each week. Coupled with the fact that a new assessment system takes three years to bed in, we are effectively target setting with jelly. But it is more than that.

Mary Jane Drummond set the challenge that if we take children's 'levels' and use them to predict future attainment we are 'colluding in a deterministic and profoundly anti-educational enterprise'. She sees that assuming what they can do today to be a predictor of where they will be tomorrow, or at the moment of the next statutory assessment, to be particularly dangerous (Swaffield, 2008, p. 11). It certainly feels like we are putting a glass ceiling on some while deciding to lift it off for others. Yes, these targets should be aspirational but it still involves deciding if each child will make it or not. We are then faced with the real and present danger that Sergei, who the teacher has classified into the group who will not make ARE, will not receive full-time attention as he is not expected to reach ARE. Some, such as Wynne Harlen, have suggested that pupils are involved in internal target setting so they are in control of the glass ceiling (Swaffield, 2008, p. 141). It seems to me that shared aspirational targets for each lesson or unit of work will automatically result in a relentless drive towards success. The need for a percentage target set for the end of the year therefore seems superfluous.

Another concern is that our school targets are frequently affected by national expectations, rather than our own internal knowledge of our children. The goal posts set by the government are forever moving so we can get caught in a permanent state of flux, with targets that we had set having to be changed due to the latest set of published data. What we had aspired for originally is suddenly not good enough as the national picture has changed again. However, if we look at performance data and target setting more as a reality check to help us with our self-evaluation and therefore inform our strategic planning, it can prove beneficial and a little less pointless.

In-school targets rely very heavily on accurate assessments. One headteacher told me they no longer saw the point of termly assessments as teachers were often over-cautious at Christmas, more likely to show change by Easter but would save the evidence of the real movement to the end of the summer term. In addition, targets are reliant on the assessments of previous teachers, either within the same school or from colleagues from other establishments. Furthermore, schools also need to be confident that a teacher's assessment of performance in the classroom also matches to how a child performs under test conditions, particularly for Key Stage 1 phonics and Key Stage 2 targets. So, when we are setting targets, schools need to be clear what their target is in – classroom performance or test performance?

Quite rightly there are now greater expectations of what pupils should be able to master by the end of their time in primary school. The idea that a child who had just crept over the Level 4 barrier was secondary ready was not ideal. All my teachers know that the expectations have increased. All my teachers are working really hard with all our pupils to make sure that they do as well as they can. Do I need to set them targets to make sure that quality teaching and learning is happening? I will come back to this in Chapter 7.

GET MONITORING

Either with or without Levels, apparently strong data on its own should not reassure all those who need to hold the school to account that all is well. Senior leaders need to get stuck in and carry out regular monitoring to ensure that any data on a spreadsheet matches what is seen in the classroom and in children's work. Is there enough evidence to prove that teacher assessments are accurate and that the picture presented by the number crunching is therefore a true one? Are standards really rising in maths? Are SEND children progressing as well as their peers? Does the quality of teaching and learning match what is in the books? No school wants to be hit with a nasty surprise when it comes to Key Stage 1 and Key Stage 2 assessments. Triangulating evidence from learning walks, work scrutiny, planning reviews (where appropriate) and pupil interviews against the ARE Performance Descriptors for each year group will give a strong indication of the position of the school and will enable more informed conversations with governors, the local authority and Ofsted.

WORKING WITH OFSTED

The thought of a visit from Ofsted feels few people with joy. While most headteachers would agree that it is right that schools are held to account by an external body, there remains concerns around inconsistencies of approach from team to team alongside the pressure of keeping up with constantly changing guidelines and Handbook updates. The weight of the importance of data in school inspections has continued to increase; the notion that the team has poured over your Raiseonline before arriving at your school to then set about proving that their presumptions were right has been the reality for many. Before the cull of inspectors in 2015, I fear that there were many who relied on data to help them make judgements in attainment and progress because they were unable to recognise it in the classroom. Possibly this is where the pressure to produce year-on-year or term-on-term tracking sheets came from. As a result, schools have been very concerned that in a life without Levels, they will be left exposed in some way.

As we move forward into a new era, it is a great opportunity for us to take control of how data is used in an Ofsted inspection. It feels like for once Ofsted are on the back foot. I do not pity them moving from school to school trying to make sense of hundreds of different assessment systems and deciding whether or not they are robust enough and effective. This is our chance to take our assessment information to them.

READ THE OFSTED GUIDANCE

Ofsted are much better now at sharing with schools the same information that they are giving to their inspectors. It therefore makes sense to read this and to be reassured by it. The latest

Handbook and Inspection Framework, which can be found on the Ofsted website, are essential reading and the 2014 guidance to inspectors regarding the inspection of schools during 2014–15 is also useful as it makes it clear what they are, and aren't, looking for (Ofsted, 2014). *The Final Report of the Commission on Assessment Without Levels* also has helpful guidance of working with Ofsted in this area (McIntosh, 2015).

KNOW YOUR DATA AS WELL AS THEY DO

- Be aware of any data that they have access to and know it as well as they will in terms of how it looks for the strengths and areas of development for the school.

- Remember that FFT data is not available to them and you do not need to give it to them.

- Be ready to share the stories of any particular children who did not make expected progress but were on track to. Be ready to share all interventions that were put in place. However, schools need to be aware that with the removal of the scale of Levels, there are no longer borderlines that children can be shown to have 'just' missed. Instead there will just be the SS.

- Have a three-year summary of the headlines from Raiseonline so you can point out where something was a one-off dip rather than a steady decline.

- Remember that they are interested in what is happening in your school now. This is especially helpful to remember when the previous year's results were a dip year.

YOU ARE IN CHARGE OF WHAT YOU HAND OVER

- Talk about the headlines in your in-house data but go straight on to say how that is backed up by evidence. This shows that you triangulate your evidence.

- Talk about trends in your data. Let the data tell an on-going story and explain what your predictions are for the future. They will want to know the headlines and then put them to test in the classroom.

- Ofsted do not need to see your tracking sheets, especially if they have large amounts of red on them. If you are going to hand them over, consider using a colour other than red for areas of concern. Second, if you are explaining your system then give them a copy of a class or cohort that you are confident with as an example. This will clarify how your assessment works without exposing the areas you would rather hold back.

- There is no point in spending hours making complex charts and graphs for something that they might not ask about. If a question is asked that you don't know the answer to then you can say you will get them that information shortly.

- Ofsted currently talk about 'performance information' (p. 24). This can include the case studies and progress portfolios discussed earlier. Don't get into the trap of only talking about data. Think in terms of all your assessments.

- Remember that with many schools having shorter, one-day inspections there will be less time for trawling through internal data and more time spent in the classrooms.

KNOW YOUR ASSESSMENT SYSTEM

- Look at the bullet points in the 2014/15 guidance for inspectors referred to above and make sure you can explain how your assessment system, or ethos, fulfils each of these.

- Make sure all members of staff and governors can talk about how it works.

- Be clear how *various* assessment information is gathered and how this feeds in *regularly* to 'plan appropriate teaching and learning strategies, including to identify pupils who are falling behind in their learning or who need additional support, enabling pupils who are falling behind in their learning or who need additional support, enabling pupils to make good progress and achieve well' (Ofsted Handbook, 2015, p. 45).

- Talk about your assessment system with pride and all that you have achieved as a school in getting to your current point. It is no mean feat to successfully incorporate a new way of assessing progress and attainment alongside a new National Curriculum.

- Equally, be prepared to talk about the glitches that you are experiencing and what you are doing to get round these.

- Have to hand evidence of how you are making your data as robust as possible so that it is as reliable as possible. Where does the evidence come from and what is the rationale that sits behind teacher assessments?

- Be ready for a conversation around target setting. The real nub of this is that Ofsted are looking for reassurance of a culture of high levels of expectation.

- Be clear on how accountability is tied in with staff appraisal.

REMEMBER THAT OFSTED WILL BE LOOKING IN CLASSROOMS

- It is all very well telling an inspector that SEND data is showing a rise in levels of attainment but the real test comes when they start to observe SEND practice in the classroom. That's where previous monitoring is so vital.

- Ofsted want to see that the level of expectation is high for all pupils and that will be wholly apparent from the content of lessons and work in books. A simple question to a child, 'Is this easy, tricky or just right?' can tell you a huge amount of information about likely levels of future progress if this snapshot is reflective of their usual diet.

- The assessment system needs to be evident in the classroom. This is where it is important to remember that assessment is not just about the data crunching in the file or on the computer. How does the school's assessment ethos permeate into the classroom? Is there a unified approach in terms of feedback? How are teachers showing that they are making and acting on assessments?

- How well do pupils show their understanding of assessment in school? When asked, the Hiltingbury Junior pupils will grab their Ladders and they are off. But we also need to make sure that they understand the bigger picture. How do children respond if asked to show a piece of feedback that has helped them with their learning? Do they recognise that Star, Step, Strategy is there to help move their learning on? Remember – presume nothing!

GOVERNORS DRIVING SCHOOL ACCOUNTABILITY

Ofsted inspectors are fairly infrequent visitors to schools but our governors are with us, for support and challenge, throughout the year. Consequently, it is essential that we make the most of this vital group of individuals to help foster a constructive climate of accountability. The role of governors has certainly changed over the decades. Original guidance, at the turn of the last century, was for governors to have, 'A general zeal for education …, residence in reasonable proximity to the school, together with leisure time during school hours' (Terry, 1988, p. 4). Yet the latest remit for governors, from Ofsted's current chief inspector, Sir Michael Wilshaw, is,

> to set the school's vision, ethos and strategic direction. They are also expected to hold the headteacher to account for the performance of teachers and pupils, and to ensure that public money is being well spent. Governors have to be perceptive people who can challenge and support the headteacher in equal measure and know when and how to do this.
>
> (Wilshaw, 2016)

Terry Bartlett promotes the notion that, 'If strategic leadership is setting the direction and ensuring we are on the right path, holding to account is its twin: asking the right questions of the right people to ensure they are doing what they are supposed to be doing to get us there' (Bartlett, 2013, p. 65). One of my own governors, Judith Rutherford, summarises her role in relation to assessment and accountability in the following way.

One of our key responsibilities as Governors is to ensure children receive the very best education possible and to help the school deliver this through appropriate support and challenge. At a strategic level this means having confidence in the quality of teaching and learning, and being able to monitor the progress and attainment of pupil cohorts as they move through the school.

With the old curriculum achievement was measured by Levels and we became familiar with consistent definitions of expected progress and attainment. We understood the quantitative data available to measure this and were able interpret that information to make judgements. Under the new curriculum, we still need clarity and confidence in the assessment method used. We must also understand the target setting process and whether our children are on track. Where this is not the case we need to know that effective interventions are in place.

In a Life after Levels the achievement expectation and method of measurement may have changed but the responsibilities we have as Governors remain the same. The challenge is to work with our schools to develop a clear understanding of how we set rigorous targets, measure progress and assess age-related expectations in this new environment. We must develop new sets of qualitative and quantitative data that can be used to effectively hold the school to account and continue to ensure the very best outcomes for children.

In a post-Levels world, where the familiarities of recognised data have gone and school assessments are in a state of flux, the temporary absence of a nationally recognised language of accountability can be unnerving. Let us consider some key ways that governors can still ensure that their support and challenge is effective in holding headteachers and senior leaders to account for the standards achieved in their school.

TRAINING

A core number of governors need to be up to speed with national changes in assessment and with the school's own assessment ethos. Attending any training the local authority might provide (Hampshire County Council are excellent at this), being involved in parent information evenings and staff CPD and remaining fully abreast of any literature released nationally are all important. Being linked with the school's Assessment Leader will also prove beneficial.

KNOW THE DATA IS RELIABLE

Just as there needs to be a balance between support and challenge, so there needs to be equilibrium between trust and rigour. Governors cannot question *every* piece of information that is put to them. However, Wilshaw warns against governors, 'who lack curiosity and are too willing to accept what they are being told about pupils' progress and the quality of teaching. As a consequence, they often hold an overly optimistic view of how the school is performing' (Wilshaw, 2016). The solution comes from knowing that any assessment information, particularly in a post-Levels world, is reliable.

- How much CPD has there been for staff on the new assessment system?

- How much training is the Assessment Leader receiving?

- What plans are in place for standardisation and moderation?

- Are we working with any colleagues from other schools to moderate our judgements?

- Is national information being used to help moderate our judgements?

- Where does the information come from that facilitates teacher judgements?

- How does the monitoring of the SLT support these judgements? How can governors get involved with this?

- What other evidence triangulates with this to show this data to be reliable?

- Is the new data telling us a very different story from the Levels data?

- Are staff being overly cautious or overly ambitious in their predictions?

- How is any new tracking system being monitored?

- Is there clear guidance on how attainment judgements, and therefore progress measures, are made?

- How are any targets being set?

Our school has been living and breathing assessment for the past couple of years but we still need to continually ask ourselves these questions.

UNDERSTAND THE LANDSCAPE

Understanding the lie of the land is all about governors asking the big questions around school performance. Is attainment in maths increasing over time? Are rates of progress stronger in reading or writing? Are rates of progress as strong for maths in Key Stage 1 as Key Stage 2? Are levels of attainment for Disadvantaged pupils looking comparative to their peers of similar starting points? Is it the children from lower prior starting points who are struggling to make expected progress? These broad statements can come from the data collected in the example pro formas suggested in Chapter 5, along with evidence from monitoring by the SLT.

Below is a summary of key questions that help governors to keep track of the big picture.

- Where are standards improving and why? What is the evidence?

- Where are standards remaining constant and why? What is the evidence? Is the status quo acceptable (e.g. standards are remaining significantly above the national average) or can we do better?

- Where are standards declining and why? What is the evidence? What interventions are already in place and are they enough? Is this a short-term issue (e.g. related to a specific cohort) or a school-wide picture?

- Is the percentage of pupils not on track getting smaller?

- What is the school's definition of good (expected) progress? Is the number of children meeting that getting larger?

- For specific groups, is their performance against their peers improving or declining? Where there are very small numbers involved, what is the picture over time?

- How well informed are subject leaders regarding the achievement of pupils in their area of the curriculum?

It is important to remind ourselves again that a very simple tracking system along with robust monitoring evidence can supply the answers to the majority of these questions. Having the maths leader, for example, come and speak to the governing body, or the link governor being involved in a learning walk or pupil interviews is so much more powerful than simply looking at a menu of graphs and percentages.

UNDERSTAND THE NATIONAL CHALLENGES

At the same time, governors need to ask how the school is coping with the impact of the following issues. These are not 'excuses' for slow performance but do need to be taken into account.

- How are we fairing against new, tougher levels of accountability? If our rates of attainment and progress are going to dip, how do we know that this is proportionate to the size of the challenge?

- What is the impact of moving from a 'best fit' approach to assessment in Early Years to a 'whole fit' approach in Key Stage 1 and Key Stage 2?

- How many children would reach ARE if the best fit model were applied rather than the whole fit? What are the domains (or Ladders) that are proving to be the stumbling blocks?

- National rates of progress for junior schools are recognised to be typically lower than that of primary schools. Junior schools need to seek ways to compare themselves with other junior schools.

- Schools with high percentages of pupils with English as an additional language often show strong rates of progress from Key Stage 1 to Key Stage 2. How are schools with lower numbers of these pupils fairing?

- How are schools going to work to show where children have 'just missed out' on achieving ARE now that the Levels thresholds are no longer there? Not every paper can be sent back for re-marking in Key Stage 2.

- Statutory assessments are high stakes. Is the curriculum suffering as a result of the pressure to get the right results at the end of key stages?

Chapter summary

- The removal of Levels has left some schools feeling vulnerable with regards to accountability as data plays a large role in how schools are judged.

- Progress information for accountability can come in a number of forms and numerical data is just one of those.

- Where there is quality teaching, learning and assessment in place, the pressure for complex tracking systems is removed.

- Schools will know more about their internal data and how it is calculated than Osted will.

- Governors can provide support and challenge around accountability all year round.

- Quality monitoring will give the most reliable information in terms of school performance.

References

Bartlett, T. (2013) *The Perfect Ofsted School Governor.* Carmarthen: The Thinking Press.

McIntosh, J. (chair) (2015) *Final Report on the Commission on Assessment Without Levels.* Department for Education and Standards and Testing Agency.

NAHT (2014) *Report of the NAHT Commission on Assessment.* Haywards Heath: NAHT.

Ofsted (2014) *Note for Inspectors: Use of assessment information during inspections in 2014/14.* London: Ofsted.

Ofsted (2015) *School Inspection Handbook.* London: Ofsted.

Ofsted (2015) *The Common Inspection Framework: Education, skills and early years.* London: Ofsted.

Swaffield, S. (ed.) (2008) *Unlocking Assessment: Understanding for reflection and application.* London: Routledge.

Terry, M. (1988) *Governing Schools: Powers, issues and practice.* London: Macmillan Education.

Wilshaw, M. (2016) *21st century governance needed for 21st century schools.* https://www.gov.uk/government/speeches/hmcis-monthly-commentary-november-2015 (Accessed 18.2.16).

Further reading

Gann, N. (2015) *Improving School Governance: How better governors make better schools.* London: Routledge.

7 ACCOUNTABILITY AND TEACHER PERFORMANCE

This chapter will:

- summarise the recent changes to teacher performance management;
- consider why data is not essential for measuring teacher performance;
- suggest alternative, data free approaches to performance management.

A NEW ERA OF TEACHER PAY

September 2014 saw the implementation of Performance Related Pay (PRP) for the teaching profession. It was a highly controversial change to the way that teachers' pay was decided and how performance management (PM) was organised. Remember the Newcastle Report discussed in Chapter 1? That approach by the Victorians to reward teachers for good test scores does not feel a million miles from where we are now. The unions argued that PRP would not help to raise standards while newspaper articles quoted various government reports stating that approximately half the teachers in Britain agreed that this new approach to agreeing pay was fairer than the previous system based on long service and, for many, an automatic pay increase at the end of most years (BBC, 2014).

The arguments for and against PRP could fill this entire chapter, if not a whole book, but that is not the purpose of our discussion here. For nearly two years now we have been working within the PRP system. What is of interest to us at this moment in time is how, or if, the move away from Levels will impact how schools manage PRP. What role does, or should, assessment data play in measuring teacher performance?

PERFORMANCE MANAGEMENT OR STAFF APPRAISAL?

Before the arrival of PRP, different schools had different systems for managing the performance of staff; some were designed primarily for supporting professional development while others focused on a system of staff appraisal. Armstrong and Baron clarify the difference between the two, although the terms are often used synonymously.

Performance management is a comprehensive, continuous and flexible approach to the management of organisations, teams and individuals which involves the maximum amount of dialogue between those concerned. Performance appraisal is a more limited approach which involves managers making top-down assessments and rating the performance of sub-ordinates at an annual performance appraisal meeting.

(Armstrong and Baron, 2007, p. 14)

Now that schools are running PRP, it feels as if there is a need for both approaches to run simultaneously. The end-of-year appraisal is clearly necessary as the result of this 'final assessment' informs the pay decision. It is the ultimate 'pass or fail' decision. Yet it is imperative that we keep the richness, discourse and reflection of the professional development that PM facilitates. In keeping with the theme of the book, we could make a crude comparison and say that appraisal is a summative assessment while PM is more formative. For this chapter I will refer only to PM, but recognising this as combining the two elements. Much of what I say in this chapter also applies to teaching support staff but I will focus on teachers here.

WHAT HAS PERFORMANCE MANAGEMENT GOT TO DO WITH LIFE AFTER LEVELS?

During my research for this chapter I read numerous articles relating to PRP in teaching and every single one that I looked at made a connection between performance and test results. There was a clear message, from within the profession and from outside it, that teacher success is reflected by data. You know from Chapter 6 how much concern that there has been on the removal of Levels and the potential problems it has posed around issues of accountability. It has been the same for PRP. If Levels are removed, how are schools to measure teacher performance?

I absolutely disagree with this. For the past two years at Hiltingbury we have not set data-based targets or objectives for teachers' performance management. We have looked at where data might be a useful piece of evidence to support a specific target (more on that later) but we have not set a target which is solely focused on securing particular levels of pupil attainment or progress. Initially this was because we were moving to a new assessment system and we felt that we would be setting and measuring targets with jelly. While the system had some form it was not yet solid enough to support other processes. However, even though we now have a more developed assessment system with which to replace Levels, we have chosen not to return to this. There is strength in the Industry in Education's (IIE) report *Milestone or Millstone? Performance Management in Schools*, that comments, 'it would be difficult to argue that pupil achievement should have no place in a consideration of teacher performance'

(Reeves et al., 2002, p. 43). However, how *pupil* achievement is measured can come in a variety of formats, as can *teacher* achievement.

Feeling rather paranoid that perhaps ours was the only school in the country not to be panicking about the loss of Levels to measure teacher performance, I went to check what current guidance there is from the DfE. There is the *School Teachers' Pay and Conditions Document 2015 and Guidance on School Teachers' Pay and Conditions*, published September 2015 and also the *Implementing Your School's Approach to Pay* guidance from the same month. Having read through both of these I am reassured that at no point are there statutory instructions laid out for the setting of data-based targets, relating to test scores or any other assessment sources. The latter document gives some clear points for schools to consider and those relevant to our discussion are set out below.

- Schools need to ensure that their pay policies are clear that performance related progression provides the basis for all decisions on pay – for classroom teachers and leaders. (page 5)

- It is up to each school to decide for itself how best to implement the arrangements and develop its policies accordingly. (page 5)

- Appraisal should be a supportive, developmental process designed to ensure that all teachers have the skills and support they need to carry out their role effectively. It should help to ensure that teachers continue to improve their professional practice throughout their careers. (page 7)

- Assessment may be based on evidence from a range of sources – for example, self-assessment, peer review, tracking pupil progress, lesson observations, the views of pupils and parents. (page 8)

- Headteachers will need to set out what it is they will take into account in making judgements about whether teachers have met their objectives and the relevant standards. This might include: impact on pupil progress; impact on wider outcomes for pupils; improvements in specific elements of practice, such as behaviour management or lesson planning; impact on effectiveness of teachers or other staff; wider contribution to the work of the school. (page 8)

So, schools do not have to set their teaching staff data-based targets. Instead, headteachers need to ensure that the targets that are set ultimately add to the improvement of outcomes for pupils, either in their own class or within the wider picture of the school.

We could end the chapter at this point, arguing that as data and assessment evidence is not required in PRP then there is no need to worry about accountability with life after Levels! However, while we are here, let us consider how PM can work productively in a post-Levels world.

DOUBLE TAKE ON USING DATA

Just as schools would be concerned if their Ofsted judgement was based solely on its Raiseonline data, so too should a teacher be if data is the primary, or only, source of assessment of their performance. Having spoken to colleagues from a variety of schools and local authorities, the reality for the vast majority is that teachers have one PM target that is explicitly linked to pupil progress data, with a second usually reserved for those in leadership positions who are responsible for the rates of pupil progress outside of their own class. While this might account for only a third or quarter of targets set, it is still worth considering how helpful and fair this is.

THE RELIABILITY OF THE DATA

Within a primary school, the vast majority of pupil progress data is going to come from teacher assessments. An outsider from a different industry would want to question the sense in this. They might liken this to someone working on a customer service desk writing their own client reviews. While we all want to trust in our colleagues and believe that they are willing and able to make accurate judgements, will it always be the case that the percentages of MA EXC they report are totally accurate? However, there will also be errors from over-enthusiastic assessing and when that is compared with those assessments from a colleague who has been overly cautious then the reliability of the data for PRP purposes has to be questioned. Schools also need to be clear around potential inconsistencies of approach if they take teacher assessments for some groups but the statutory assessments for others. Should a Year 6 teacher, for example, be held to account for the maths results from the SATs test while the Year 4 teacher submits their teacher assessments for maths for scrutiny?

Currently, there is also the issue of schools getting to grips with new assessment systems. Levels and APS provided a national language with an extensive system of resources for moderation. Excitingly, schools are now building their own alternatives. But it seems unreasonable that while this takes place and judgements are understandably less reliable that data should play such a major part in the setting of PRP targets. To give further weight to this, the DfE has clarified that no school should face intervention as a result of 2016 data alone. If that is the case for schools then it must be the same for our teachers.

CHILDREN ARE ALL SO DIFFERENT

It must also be remembered that not all classes pose an equal challenge in terms of setting data targets around progress. For those schools who still have sets, the teacher who is working with the lower current attainers is likely to have to work more creatively, skilfully and with greater exertion than their colleague with the higher current attainers teaching maths down the corridor to maintain equal levels of progress. Differences such as these must be taken into account.

PUPIL ACHIEVEMENT IS A CULMINATION OF TEACHING OVER TIME

Yes, teachers can be set data targets that start from a baseline when pupils arrive in their class and are then based on the school's recognised expected levels of progress during the course of a year. But any assessment made on pupil achievement reflects the culmination of their educational experience to that point. For example, one child may have moved from class to class, having the highest-performing teachers year on year. They are in a much better place to grab the curriculum and get learning than their peers who have not been so fortunate. Their more limited educational experiences mean that their current learning power may not be comparable. It will potentially be harder for the teacher of the latter pupils to get them to make expected progress than the teacher of the former pupil.

WHAT MESSAGE DOES A DATA TARGET GIVE TO TEACHING STAFF?

Some have observed that, 'improving performance management can be viewed crudely as "getting them to pull their socks up" on the assumption that with good control mechanisms and sufficient pressure staff will perform better' (Reeves et al., 2002, p. 2). Equally, just as we observed that in the past there was a potential over-reliance of Ofsted inspectors on data to help measure the quality of teaching and learning, I wonder if this has also been the case in schools for PM from headteachers. The notion of data-based targets sending a clear message of expectations while also giving no-nonsense evidence of whether teaching and learning was up to standard would have appealed to many senior leaders.

BUT I ONLY TEACH THEM TWO DAYS A WEEK!

Part-time teachers are very much part of the professional landscape. When it comes to PRP, the lack of perceived autonomy for the achievements of the pupils they teach can be a cause for concern for that teacher, or their colleagues. There is a potential issue where there is greater autonomy around pupil achievement for full-time staff compared to part-time staff when their PRP is more intrinsically tied up with the performance of other professionals. Some schools set data targets regardless, while others look to give them smaller groups of children for them to focus on. Some schools have avoided setting a data-based target for these members of staff, which has caused friction with those who are full time.

THE LOSS OF THE DETAIL OF APS

We have talked at length comparing the breadth of Performance Descriptors, such as WT or WW ARE, to the smaller steps of APS, and how these have been relied upon to give indications of movement through the National Curriculum. There are many who are looking to break down such descriptors into neat chunks simply to satisfy the need for measuring progress rates and therefore give a neat solution to tracking and accountability measures, including PRP. This is simply creating APS by another name. The teaching profession does not need to spend its time creating numerical measures to prove that teachers are teaching and learners are learning.

AN ALTERNATIVE APPROACH TO PERFORMANCE MANAGEMENT

WORKING PARTIES

For the past two years at Hiltingbury we have run PM working parties. These are open to all teachers with the purpose of reviewing how we are going to structure the PM process in the coming year. We are seeking to ensure that we invest in the professional development of teachers as well as setting out clear guidance on how PRP judgements will be made. We debate what is best practice and current thinking in terms of measuring teacher performance and agree how targets should be shaped and assessed. If we have complete ownership of this as a team then I feel confident as headteacher that the process is valued by all and perceived to be fair. We need to be in agreement about the different ways that there are to measure teacher performance and pupil performance.

TRIANGULATING EVIDENCE

Previously, one PM target was focused around pupil progress, perhaps in the form of an APS target for the class in reading, writing and maths. As already stated, this is a practice that we no longer do. Instead, we set a target based around quality of teaching in line with the teaching standards. We agree what the success criteria for this will be and the sorts of evidence that a teacher might wish to use in support of their achievement. Data can be one of these and the teacher is involved in setting the parameters for any data-based evidence. We are not saying that data is irrelevant, only that it should be seen as part of the bigger picture. The success criteria might be to triangulate four pieces of evidence to support achievement of the target. As long as the target is SMART (specific, measurable, attainable, relevant and time-limited) then the supporting evidence can be varied. This could be in the form of lesson visits, pupil interviews, planning scrutiny where appropriate, discussions with the teacher, evidence of wider reading and its impact, notes from coaching or mentoring sessions, work sampling or parent information evenings run and the associated evaluations.

REMOVAL OF FORMAL LESSON OBSERVATIONS

Rather than the termly lesson observation, we now run weekly learning walks. They are announced on the day and a member of the headship team will be in each class for anything from five to twenty minutes, depending on what is going on. The objective is to build up a picture over time if the teaching and learning in each room is meeting or exceeding expectation, rather than just witnessing 'show lessons'. The response from teaching staff has been very positive although some were slightly nervous to begin with. The open door culture already established in the school means that people coming and going from your classroom feels perfectly normal. The member of staff conducting the visit gets stuck into the lesson, talking with the children and acting as an extra pair of hands. As a monitoring exercise it is used to feed *in* and feed *back*. The information gathered *feeds into* the on-going evaluation of the school and helps inform future decisions, such as the programme for CPD. There is also the chance to *feed back* on a regular basis either to individuals or to groups and facilitate discussion. If there is cause for concern from these regular visits then that will be addressed in the agreed manner.

INVEST TIME INTO THE PROCESS

PM is an incredibly powerful tool to help schools develop and grow. Much of this power comes from the sense of value that teachers feel when they know that the school is genuinely investing in them. PM cannot be seen merely as a tick box exercise.

- Run two separate meetings for PM in October. The first should be an hour to enable quality discussions to review the previous targets. This gives the teacher the chance to share all that they have done and to really unpick their professional development over the course of the year. It requires evidence to be shared and looked at properly. At Hiltingbury, all these sessions take place with the headteacher. The second meeting is then with a member of the headship team to set the new targets. These targets are moderated to ensure consistency of expectation.

- Target setting needs to balance driving whole school priorities and supporting teachers' ownership of areas to focus on.

- Provide short termly review sessions, with a member of SLT, to discuss where they are with their targets, clear up any misconceptions that they might have and to ensure that they are confident with the types of evidence that they will need to produce to show that their target has been achieved.

- Where staff are happy, share key targets that have been adopted so teachers can work collaboratively with others who are working on similar areas.

- Ensure that additional CPD is available if required. This might come in the form of whole staff training, courses or conferences, coaching or mentoring, visits to watch other colleagues or time for professional reading.

- Where funding permits, providing a Golden Day for professional development can be really beneficial. This is a day for staff to use as they see best to help with their professional development. It could be spent visiting other schools, working in a research library, carrying out wider reading, conducting pupil interviews or observing colleagues teach.

Chapter summary

- Schools need to ensure that their PM systems support PRP.
- The investment in performance development should not be lost in the accountability of PRP.
- There are various ways to measure teacher performance, beyond just data.
- Data as an evidence source has its limitations.
- There are other non-data based sources of evidence that are equally valuable.
- The removal of Levels should have no impact on the quality of PRP and PM provided in schools.

References

Armstrong, M. and Baron, A. (2007) *Managing Performance: Performance management in action.* London: CIPD.

BBC (2014) 'Link pay to pupil progress, over half of teachers polled say' http://www.bbc.co.uk/news/education-27722356 (Accessed 5.3.16).

Department for Education (2015) *Implementing Your School's Approach to Pay.* London: Department for Education.

Department for Education (2015) *School Teachers' Pay and Conditions Document 2015 and Guidance on School Teachers' Pay and Conditions.* London: Department for Education.

Reeves, R., Forde, C., O'Brien, J., Smith, P. and Tomlinson, H. (2002) *Performance Management in Education: Improving practice.* London: Paul Chapman.

Further reading

Corby, S., Palmer, S. and Lindop, E. (ed.) (2009) *Rethinking Reward.* Basingstoke: Palgrave Macmillan.

Simons, H. and Elliott, J. (ed.) (1989) *Rethinking Appraisal and Assessment*. Milton Keynes: Open University Press.

Tauman, P. (2009) *Teaching by Numbers: Deconstructing the discourse of standards and accountability in Education*. Abingdon: Routledge.

Trethowan, D. (1991) *Managing With Appraisal: Achieving quality schools through performance management*. London: Paul Chapman.

Turner, G. and Clift, P. (1988) *Studies in Teacher Appraisal*. Lewes: The Falmer Press.

PART FOUR
ASSESSMENT TOOLKIT

8 IDEAS AND STRATEGIES FOR PRIMARY ASSESSMENT

> This section of the book will:
>
> • offer some practical suggestions for capturing assessment evidence in the classroom;
> • share tried and tested strategies for promoting a positive assessment culture;
> • suggest possible additions to your assessment arsenal to develop or extend your current practice.

This final chapter of the book aims to provide as many practical ideas and suggestions as possible to support quality assessment, both formative and summative, in the classroom. It is a collection of great practice and clever ideas that I have collected over many years. Background reading and developing professional knowledge is essential, but picking up a golden nugget or two of practical suggestions that can make an immediate impact in your classroom is always exciting.

The source of these ideas includes courses and conferences that I have attended, books I have read, strategies I have seen happening when I have visited other classes and schools, ideas people have told me about over a coffee and suggestions from colleagues and pupils. There are even a few that I came up with myself! Where I have been so careful throughout the book to attribute all thinking and quotes to individuals and authors through the references, this chapter is slightly more problematic. The thought of plagiarism is not appealing but for many ideas I simply cannot recall where the idea came from, or have heard it from several sources. As teachers we are the ultimate magpies. Therefore, I am offering up the contents of my nest, acknowledging that I am not the original owner of all I offer here. Having said that, I expect some of those owners weren't the original creators either!

Two recent books that I would recommend are *Engaging Learners* and *Teaching Backwards*, both by Andy Griffith and Mark Burns. I have included a few of their ideas here but the books are well worth a read as they contain a wealth of practical ideas for teaching and learning in the classroom.

The practical suggestions that follow are in some sort of order. However, many of them would fit in more than one section. It might be that your school is using all these techniques, but hopefully there will be something in here for everybody.

8.1 GETTING EVIDENCE FROM THE CHILDREN IN THE CLASSROOM

Offer three or four multiple choice answers and allocate a corner of the classroom for each of these. The children need to **vote with their feet**. Get a teaching assistant (TA) or a pupil to capture the evidence by taking a photograph. The questioning can be repeated to make a knock-out game. Children can play as individuals or pairs.

The above can be achieved with children remaining in their seats but instead with a set of **multiple choice cards**, A to D. Colour coding makes it easier for the adult to pick out which letters have been selected but having them all the same colour makes it harder for those who are unsure to simply follow the crowd.

A great technological version of the above is **Plickers**. Currently free, this is a web-based app. Each child in the class has a printed card which is unique to them with a shape in the centre. Each side of the shape is labelled with A to D. When given a multiple choice question, the children hold up their shape in the correct orientation for their answer. The teacher or TA then scans the cards with a mobile device and the data is stored. It can either be shared in real time with the children or used summatively or formatively by the teacher. The A to D letters are very small so it prevents children copying what others are saying.

Give each child three **coloured cups**, usually red, amber and green (RAG). As the children are working, they have the coloured cups stacked next to them with the top cup, or colour, representing their current level of confidence or how they feel they are doing against the SC. The teacher can see at a glance if there is a sea of green or red and then adjust their teaching accordingly. I am sure I saw this on a TV programme with Dylan Wiliam.

Use RAG with **marking trays** for the end of the lesson. Children select which tray to place their work, reflecting their self-assessment of their performance. I always used to start marking the red tray and end with the green.

Use body parts to get children to indicate their self-assessment against SC. I use **heads, shoulders and knees** rather than thumbs up or down as it is more explicit and they have to get off the fence when deciding.

Ask children to **choose their position on the carpet**, depending on their self-assessment of how confident they feel. If the most confident are further back then it also makes it easier for them to leave the carpet if they are ready to move on.

Place round the room a selection of answers, solutions, suggestions or approaches. Provide each child with five **sticky dots**. They need to place three dots by their first choice, two by their second and one by their third. If sticky dots seem too daunting then a coloured pencil is an alternative.

At the end of the session, give each child an **exit pass** question, differentiated where appropriate. They need to write their answer down and hand it in as they leave. They can be given out on arrival so that they know what it is they are going to need to be able to answer before they leave the classroom.

Quizzes and tests are a great way to capture assessment information quickly. Teachers need to make sure they are clear what they are doing with the evidence this generates, or what they want the pupils to do with it. Get the children to compete table to table or classroom to classroom to make it into a game.

Try **Coin Tosser** as a way to add spice to a quiz. Get children in pairs swatting up for a mini quiz at the end of a session or unit. Just before the test, toss a coin to see which of the two is going to take the quiz on behalf of both them. The results will be shared! (Keeling, 2009, p. 126)

Non-stop quizzes involve children running to an adult for the question, getting back to their place to work out the answer and then going back to the teacher to share the answer and receive the next question. The teacher can differentiate on the spot and start to give them harder or easier questions in real time. The class can decide how this is to be scored.

Children writing a quiz is win win as the teacher gets double the assessment data, from both the quality of the quiz written and how successfully it is completed.

Make use of any **online quiz writing** tool as it will store the data and usually do the marking too! Hiltingbury uses the various tools on Google Apps for Schools.

Pupil conferences are time consuming but worthwhile. Fifteen minutes with a child drilling into a key area, such as reading or learning behaviours, can provide essential assessment information.

Make use of the 'A' in planning, preparation and assessment time (PPA). **PPA** is a great time to carry out some assessments with pupils or small groups. Alternatively, get someone else to teach your class so you can get stuck in with assessing.

Ask children to prepare a **presentation** for the end of a lesson or unit.

Arrested development is an end of lesson exercise where the teacher asks the children, 'If you were arrested for having learned something this lesson, would there be enough evidence to convict you – yes or no?' (Keeling, 2009, p. 121).

At the end of a lesson, split the children into small groups and get them to act out what has happened in the lesson in two minutes in an **instant replay** (Keeling, 2009, p. 117).

Set up children as **Learning Detectives**, with cameras, video recorders or microphones, and get them to capture evidence of learning on your behalf during the lesson.

8.2 MAKING THE MOST OF WALTS AND SC

Make sure the WALT is a **transferable skill**. Ask the children to tell you other contexts that they will use this in. (Maths is trickier for this and sometimes the WALT is non-transferable.)

Don't presume learners see the link between the WALT and the SC.

Ask children if they know **what they are learning**, not what they are doing, and how they will know if they have been successful.

Train parents to ask their child what they learned today rather than what they did.

Keep referring back to the WALT and the SC so that it is really embedded within the lesson. Can the children shout it, whisper it or sing it like an opera star?

Get children to **correct poor SC** that don't match the WALT so that the link between the two becomes explicit. Equally, getting the pupils to **write the SC** has the same affect.

Give them three or four sets of potential SC and get them to **rank them** in order of their relevance to the WALT.

Link questions to the SC and make pupils aware which part of the SC you are probing them on.

Label work that is on display with the SC to make it clear why it is being celebrated.

Use up-to-date working walls to **gather examples against the SC**, but make sure that pupils know this is a great place to go to help them with their learning rather than seeing this as wallpaper.

Get children to **order pieces of work using the SC** and say why. This can be made easier if they are very different levels or harder if the pieces of work are more comparable.

Where needed, **give children examples** next to the SC in a grid to ensure they know what they mean.

Use **prove-it partners** or **prove-it spaces** against the SC so that children have to use the SC.

Use a **visualiser**, scanned copies or a digital camera to get children's work on display for peer assessment against the SC.

Play **SC bingo** at the end of a session. If a child calls bingo they can only win if they have the evidence in their work.

Rewrite/re-perform the work removing the SC and get the children to see what is left.

Get the children to **film** themselves for next year's students with top tips as to how to use the SC, give examples and share what happens when SC are not used.

Put them into small groups and number them 1 to 4. Ask for evidence against SC from a member of the teams. An example might be, 'I want to see a simile from number 3s'. The **fastest to demonstrate their evidence** to the teacher wins a point for their team. This could be interesting in a music lesson!

8.3 PROMOTING PUPIL SELF-ASSESSMENT IN LESSONS TO GUIDE THEIR NEXT STEPS

Marking stations, marking booklets or answer envelopes are all ways to enable children to check after a few questions if they are getting them right without needing to wait for an adult to tell them. If they are, then can move on to something harder. If they are getting it wrong, they need to move to an easier challenge or seek support. Children take this very seriously and it is very rare that it encourages cheating.

Open-ended learning, such as investigations, can be supported with **clue cards** in envelopes that the children can access as prompts if they are struggling and need a push in the right direction. They are there if and when they decide to use them.

Many teachers now give children a **choice of challenge** rather than dictating their starting point. However, the levels of challenge and the reasons why one is harder than another need to be explained explicitly to children so they can make an informed choice rather than just being told that one is easier than the other.

Using the SC, pupils assess their work with colour pencils, one for each of the SC. They are looking for a **blaze of colour** in their book.

Get children who feel that they have finished their work and included all the SC to carry out **pupil moderation** together. Are the two pieces comparable against the SC?

At the start of the lesson, show an example of what you are going to be teaching today, or What A Good One Looks Like (WAGOLL). Ask the children if they need to stay for whole class input. If they feel they don't, **let them get on** and make a start. If they are sat in their place struggling they will naturally tune back into the teacher's delivery so all will not be lost.

Rather than finding features of a particular genre, compare a WAGOLL and What a Bad One Looks Like (WABOLL) and play spot the difference.

Make sure that children know that if they are coming to join a carpet club, either because it has been suggested by the teacher or through their self-assessment, **they can leave at any point** once they are back on track.

Video yourself or the TA explaining the next step for more confident learners so they cut away from the main class input and have their own mini teacher.

Get the children to complete a simple **Venn diagram of evidence**, with the two intersecting circles labelled as 'my work' and 'exemplar work'. The aim is to get as much evidence into the central interlocking section as possible (Griffith and Burns, 2014, p. 118).

8.4 QUALITY QUESTIONING AND DISCUSSION

Plan at least two questions you want to ask that lesson. Teachers ask hundreds of questions every day and they certainly can't all be planned. However, they can't all be made up on the spot. Great questions require great subject knowledge and a clear idea of what you want the answer to tell you. Think where you are going to record the answers.

Bloom's taxonomy is a great resource for structuring questions. There are hundreds of examples on the internet of key question structures that support each level of Bloom's pyramid. Keep a few from each section to hand and use them as a prompt to ensure your questions span every level. As you move further up the pyramid the curve ball questions discussed in Chapter 3 really come into play.

Research has shown that the more actively involved children are in their learning, the smarter they become. Therefore, teachers need to make sure that as many children as possible are as actively involved as possible. **Random generators** are a great replacement for hands-up. There are many interactive versions on the internet, such as classtools.net, which provide ways to keep children on their toes. If teachers want more control then named lolly sticks do the trick. Colour coding them (avoiding red, amber and green) enables teachers to set a question and then select a name from the pot, or the stick can be chosen and then the question decided on. The child might be asked for a suggestion, an answer, to repeat what the last person said or to add to it.

I went to a Dylan Wiliam conference on questioning several years ago and he talked about, '**pose, pause, pounce, bounce**'. The teacher must pose the question and then pause properly to allow thinking time. This thinking time needs to be longer than the two seconds that we normally give. Then there is the pounce, which is to select someone to respond, rather than responding to hands-up. The key then is to 'bounce' the answer on. Rather than evaluate the response and close the discussion down, this is the time to turn to another learner and ask them their opinion or to develop it further.

When a question has been responded to, ask the next learner if they want to respond with an '**and' or a 'but**' to show if they are agreeing and building on what has been said or challenging it in some way.

Get discussions going by **spreading rumours** round the classroom. For example, 'Why did Tom refuse to do as his aunt and uncle told him?' The children respond by whispering to each other, 'Well I heard…'

Get children to work in pairs or small groups and get their ideas or suggestions on paper. After a period of time they screw the ball up into a **snowball** and throw it to another table in the room. This can be repeated as many times as it takes to capture all the ideas – or as long as you can cope with it!

Which questions will you be asking yourself as you speak to pupils that will **prove progress**? Get that assessment book out as a prompt to remind you to assess actively.

Leave the lesson on a **cliff-hanger** and give the answer to a key question at the start of the next lesson.

Don't ask **too many questions**, especially ones you all **already know the answers** to.

Don't be too quick to **rephrase or repeat questions** when children do not respond immediately. It can confuse the learner and if you are seeking to make an assessment neither you nor they will know where they are.

If children answer, 'I don't know' ask them what they would say if they did know. Give them **multiple choice options** to build their confidence with simply replying. Talk about **great wrong answers** and ensure there is a culture of safety in being wrong.

Questioning can provide so much assessment evidence so ensure that it is not all lost. Use other adults or children as **learning detectives** to capture as much as possible. Whiteboards are great for quick responses but '**whiteboard books**' have the advantage of capturing answers for future reference, both for the teacher and the learner.

8.5 FEEDBACK

Ensure the children **appreciate the different forms that feedback comes in** and what its purpose is. Can they answer the following question reasonably swiftly? 'Can you show me/tell me about a piece of feedback that your teacher has given you that helped to move your learning on?'

Response to feedback needs **planned time** to show that it is valued. This does mean, though, that the feedback must be worth acting on. Do not tolerate learners not acting on the feedback. It needs to be recognised as a priority.

Get a clear, but manageable, system of **coloured pens** going on for feedback and response and make sure that it's stuck to. I have seen teachers use 'tickled pink' to identify success and 'green for growth' for next steps. Pupils also need colours for composing, editing and responding.

Ensure the feedback **comes at the right time**. If it always comes at the end of the unit there is no time to act on it and the impact is lost.

Hiltingbury uses **Star, step, strategy**. The biggest challenge is to ensure that the next step and the suggested strategy address the most important thing to ensure the learner makes maximum progress the next lesson.

Get the children to **evaluate the teacher's feedback**. Is it relevant and will it move the learning on?

Matching the feedback to the work is a great way to see if learners can recognise how feedback links with the WALT and the SC. Teachers need to give the work back to a small group with each piece of feedback on a separate piece of paper. The group need to re-pair the work with the feedback (Griffith and Burns, 2014, p. 249). An alternative to this is to share a piece of work with the children on the board and then give them various pieces of feedback and they can decide which apply, which don't, which would be the most helpful in moving the learning on, etc. The piece of work could be a photo or film as well as pages from a book.

Avoid rhetorical questions in feedback and definitely avoid questions that can be answered with a yes or no!

Books should **reflect the voice of the teacher and the pupil**. Getting a dialogue going in their books is great evidence to children that their work is really being looked at and therefore encourages them to continue to invest in their learning. It also creates more assessment evidence.

There needs to be a **long-term expectation of the impact of feedback**. The pupil must understand that the next steps don't just apply to the next lesson but to the rest of the work that they do after that. Build in 'prove it' time for children to show evidence of their response to feedback over a half term. Points and prizes can be awarded wherever they have done this.

Remember the **power of verbal feedback**, especially with younger children. However, ensure that children are valuing it as much as the adults do by using the scaffolds used in written feedback to cue them in. For example, a member of staff at Hiltingbury could say, 'Your star is …, your step is … and your strategy is …' Agree as a school what will be recorded in work where verbal feedback has been given.

Train children to peer assess against the SC so that their feedback is relevant. Identifying next steps and suggesting ways to get there is an amazing learning skill to have and benefits both the worker and the assessor. Foundation subjects provide a great training ground for this.

Have a **peer marking agreement** within the classroom so that peer assessment takes place in a safe environment (Griffith and Burns, 2014, p. 244).

Look to **peer assess on sticky notes** or pro formas rather than writing straight into someone's book. Some children can struggle to have the writing of another child on their work.

Feedback galleries facilitate more than one peer providing feedback as the class can move between pieces of work to evaluate progress (Griffith and Burns, 2014, p. 251).

Show you **value peer feedback** by making it form part of the weekly rota of marking. If learners are competent in this area then the teacher should not have to go back each time there is peer marking and add a teacher comment too.

8.6 PRACTICAL TIPS FOR USING LEARNING LADDERS

This section has been written by Diana Massa, our Assessment Leader, and is for those of you who are using either the Ladders booklets, or similar, with your children, the online Learning Ladders or Ladders at Home.

Invest in **reusable translucent sticky arrows** (we get ours from Asda!) that children can use to identify rungs they are currently working on that lesson or week.

Children should be encouraged to **identify the Ladder and/or rung** the lesson relates to, ensuring they really know what each of the skills mean, rather than the teacher just telling them.

Keep making reference to the Ladder skills throughout the day; for example, in history when you are reading from a range of sources you might refer to their Comprehender skills.

If children are handing in books for marking along with their Ladder booklet, get the children to **pair them up** before they hand them in, ideally slotted together at the appropriate pages.

For **younger children** or non-readers, tell them that you have signed off rungs and why and get them to colour in the sub-rung with you so they can see it grow.

If you are using the booklets and the online system, **put a dot under any sub-rungs** that have been updated on the system so the inputter knows they have already been done.

Colour in completed sub-rungs in the colour of the year group the child is in, rather than the year group the rung belongs to, thus giving a quick picture of how close a child is to ARE.

Use a **date stamp** to speed up signing off rungs.

Do as many **live sign-offs** as possible with the children in lessons, particularly Guided Reading. The children love it and it is an efficient use of time.

Focus on a couple of tables a day for assessing against a particular rung.

Teachers/TAs sign off rungs rather than children but they do the colouring.

Maths prove-it questions a couple of weeks later are a great way to gather evidence quickly, particularly if you capture and store evidence using Plickers.

Use **spelling dictations** to gather evidence for Super Speller rather than trawling through their books.

Make reference to the rungs to be assessed on **lesson plans** and then put the initials of children who have met the expectation next to them, or initials and a cross if they have not. This captured evidence can be used to update rungs at a future date.

Use the **online gap analysis** to see at a glance which rungs have not been achieved so you can focus on teaching these skills or including more questions on them.

Make use of their upcoming Guided Reading packs. These are teacher guides for quality texts along with a pupil pack. All of the questions are linked to Ladders and/or rungs and have standardised answers to ensure accurate pitch and assessment. Simply record the initial of a child next to an answer to create evidence for signing off rungs at a later date.

Chapter summary

- Assessment is so much more than a tracking system.
- Assessment strategies work hand in hand with developing learning skills and metacognition.
- Assessment in the classroom can be so much fun!

References

Griffith, A. and Burns, M. (2014) *Teaching Backwards*. Carmarthen: Crown House Publishing.

Keeling, D. (2009) *Rocket Up Your Class*. Carmarthen: Crown House Publishing.

Further reading

Beere, J. (2010) *The Perfect Ofsted Lesson*. Carmarthen: Independent Thinking Press.

Clarke, S. (2001) *Unlocking Formative Assessment: Practical strategies for enhancing pupils' learning in the primary classroom.* London: Hodder and Stoughton.

Clarke, S. (2005) *Formative Assessment in Action: Weaving the elements together.* London: Hodder Education.

Clarke, S. (2008) *Active Learning Through Formative Assessment*. London: Hodder Education.

Griffiths, A. and Burns, M. (2012) *Engaging Learners*. Carmarthen: Crown House Publishing.

Hall, K. and Burke, W. (2003) *Making Formative Assessment Work: Effective practice in the primary classroom*. Maidenhead: Open University Press.

CONCLUSIONS: TAKING CONTROL OF ASSESSMENT

Congratulations, you have made it all the way through! Or perhaps you are a flicker, and have skimmed and scanned your way to this point. Or maybe you are a dipper and have just read the chapters that were most relevant to you and have stumbled on the conclusion by chance. Either way, I hope that you have found in these pages something of use.

At the very start of the book, I said the content could be summed up by three words: opportunity, re-think and bravery. Let us consider each of these in turn as we draw our thoughts on assessment to a close.

OPPORTUNITY

I have used this word repeatedly throughout the book. F. Scott Fitzgerald said that, 'Our lives are defined by opportunities, even the ones we miss'. Another great quote comes from Sir Winston Churchill who warned that, 'The pessimist sees difficulty in every opportunity. The optimist sees opportunity in every difficulty'. I would hate for any of us to miss the opportunity that we have before us to do some amazing with assessment because it seems so daunting or too great a challenge.

I appreciate that there is a huge amount for each school to do. Much of this comes from the need for thinking time and professional dialogue and we all know that time is a precious resource in schools. Yet we must make the time. I have often thought if I were to open a school that would sit truly independently from all current national expectations and statutory requirements, what would it look like? Surely now is the time for each of us to ask ourselves that question and paint that picture of our ideal and then move towards achieving it as closely as we can. The removal of a statutory system of assessment, along with some increased freedoms around the content of the National Curriculum, really does help to give us the chance to move beyond dreaming.

RE-THINK

Hopefully this book has challenged you in some way to re-think your attitudes to assessment. We have to move away from our obsession with tracking and focus on the importance of more formative methods to underpin best practice in teaching and learning. The removal of Levels requires that teaching professionals must re-think their own knowledge of assessment, as well as their subject knowledge, and get back to basics of what excellent practice is.

We all get caught up on our own hamster wheels, where we are so busy carrying on with what we have always done that we have no opportunity to stop and decide if our practice is actually hitting the spot. I would challenge all of us to insist that our schools have regular assessment staff meetings, to facilitate discussions and debate around how we assess, why and who it is for. Is it *focused*, *purposeful* and *timely*?

BRAVERY

Bravery is the key. How easy it is to talk about opportunities and re-thinking how we can assess in new and innovative ways when the reality is that judgement of our school's success, and of school leaders' reputations, is so heavily tied up with summative assessment. We need to make brave decisions regarding our relationship with assessment and act on them. However, this does require each of us to reflect on what our own principles are regarding quality teaching and learning in school.

Many will have become de-skilled under the regime of Levels and the thought of simply showing progress in a child's book will seem daunting as they will no longer be confident of what progress actually looks like. For others, the security of a tracking system is a tool they have come to rely on when arguing their case with Ofsted inspectors that progress is happening in school. The most important thing is that we learn to trust our own judgement again. I have spoken to colleagues in so many schools in the past 24 months who have told me they were going to wait and see if there was to be more guidance on Life after Levels, either from the DfE or from their own local authorities. We must be brave and confident that we do know what we are doing. We might not all get it right first time (we have certainly had to revise our plans at Hiltingbury on more than one occasion) but it is better to take risks than to rely on others to do the thinking for you.

If I could be fairy-godmother and wave my magic wand, I would remove the burden of national statutory tests. Yes, we need accountability, but I would rather that I had regular visits from a school improvement partner who would spend time with me and my staff in the classroom to help us reflect on where we are and what our next steps should be; that would be formative assessment at its best. The high-pressure nature of the publication of results ensures that the breadth of the curriculum continues to be reduced, anxiety levels in teachers and pupils continue to rise and an over-reliance of summative assessment remains prevalent. Would it not be wonderful if all schools could be brave enough to promise to deliver a normal, rich curriculum, to ban booster classes and let their children sit statutory tests 'cold' in May. Any takers?

The storm of change around expected school performance will continue to rage, of that I am certain. Therefore, we need to know what our core values are and stick with them or else we will remain at the mercy of the winds of change. They should become our lighthouse, our moral compass, in all that we do. If our children are experiencing great teaching underpinned by great assessment throughout their time with us we should be confident that we can demonstrate how well they are doing, whatever the measuring stick we are presented with.

INDEX

LEARNING LADDERS

Get involved with the Learning Ladders project

The Learning Ladders system continues to evolve, driven by a passionate community of educators, students and parents.

It is an award-winning 'in-class and in-cloud' learning management tool to increase pupil engagement and progress, support teaching, and engage parents in their children's learning.

Learning Ladders is now used to improve teaching and learning in schools across the world.

To find out more visit
www.learningladders.info/sage

Quote "SAGE" for a 10% discount on your first year's membership.